国家汉办/孔子学院总部

Tongyong Shangwu Hanyu

通用商务汉语 2

主编：季 瑾

编者：（按姓氏笔画顺序排列）

李志娜 张建英 季 瑾 杨康丽

窦小力

译者：杨玉功

A General Course for Business Chinese

对外经济贸易大学出版社

University of International Business and Economics Press

中国·北京

图书在版编目（CIP）数据

通用商务汉语.2／季瑾主编. －北京：对外经济贸易大学出版社，2010

ISBN 978-7-81134-674-9

Ⅰ. ①通… Ⅱ. ①季… Ⅲ. ①商务-汉语-对外汉语教学-教材 Ⅳ. ①H195.4

中国版本图书馆CIP数据核字（2010）第064354号

通用商务汉语 2

A General Course for Business Chinese 2

季　瑾　主编

责任编辑：戴　菲

对 外 经 济 贸 易 大 学 出 版 社

北京市朝阳区惠新东街10号　　邮政编码：100029

邮购电话：010-64492338　　发行部电话：010-64492342

网址：http://www.uibep.com　　E-mail:uibep@126.com

唐山市润丰印务有限公司 印装　　新华书店北京发行所发行

成品尺寸：210mm×280mm　　10.5 印张　　192 千字

2010 年 05 月北京第 1 版　　2010 年 05 月第 1 次印刷

ISBN：978-7-81134-674-9

印数：0 000 － 3 000 册　　定价：38.00 元（含光盘）

前 言

《通用商务汉语》（1～3）是以培养学习者商务汉语交际能力为目标的商务汉语综合教材。本系列教材适用于海内外有一定汉语水平（相当于HSK成绩三级或以上水平）的人士的商务汉语学习。本系列教材采用场景式的编排，既便于多媒体商务汉语教学使用，也可为依附于网络平台的远程商务汉语教育服务。

一、教材的基本结构

《通用商务汉语》第一册共有6个单元，每单元有2～3篇课文，共有13篇课文；第二册共有6个单元，每单元有2篇课文，共有12篇课文；第三册共有6个单元，每单元有1～3篇课文，共有12篇课文。每个单元包括课文、生词、专有名词、注释、练习。每篇课文均配有拼音和英译文，生词和注释均为中英文对照。每册书附赠配套的光盘。

二、教材的编写特点

1．题材的实用性和针对性

本系列教材是针对各类商务汉语学习者的商务交际活动来编写的，强调融专业知识背景、工作技能以及语言基础学习为一体，不再是一些经济类报刊、新闻的简单搜集汇编，而是从语言和商务专业两方面给学习者提供系统、新颖、实用的“汉语+商务知识”的交际及工作使用语言的学习。

本系列教材的语法教学是为商务内容的学习服务，语法项目的讲解是为了帮助学习者学习商务内容时扫除语言上的障碍。注释中的语法按照其在课文中出现的顺序排列，以例句和通俗的表述来展现。此外，注释中还有习惯用法、口语中的常用语、文化知识、商务常识等方面的介绍。

本系列教材的练习包括语言结构功能训练和商务内容训练两部分。语言结构功能训练是为学习者熟悉、掌握教材中的汉语词汇和句型而设计的，适可而止，学习者会用即可。练习的类型各课基本一致，题型基本固定，前后练习统一，体现出训练的系统性。但也注意到了一些语言点的不同，在少数课后的题型上作了调整。

商务内容训练，此部分从听说读写四个方面全方位地训练学习者商务汉语交际能力，包括分角色朗读课文、阅读理解、角色扮演、完成任务等商务交际和任务训练。

2．内容的商务化

教材的内容着重商务话题下应知应会的商务常识的普及。三册教材的18个单元即为18个商务专题，每个专题下各有2～3个不同方面的课程内容。内容通过场景的编写相互关联，以扩大学生的各个商务领域的信息量为驱动，建立并扩大学生相关方面可懂信息的储存，为学习者构建一个商务常识信息平台。

在商务常识的学习中，既有社会交往，也有热门话题，题材涉及商务参观、商务接待、商务谈判、贸易流程、职场、企业管理模式和企业文化、商务招标、商务代理、市场调研、营销理念和广告、投资、商标法、知识产权、广交会、理财等。

在内容上，还根据商务交流的需要配置了一些真实的商务图表、合同、信用证、信件、求职简历、招聘广告、招标流程、代理协议、调查问卷等。

3. 体例和练习设计的交际性和任务化

本系列教材的课文是以几位核心的海内外商务人士参与商务活动为主线，以情景对话的形式来传达商务知识，在真实的商务交际场景中来学习商务汉语。

练习的重点在商务内容训练，分层次逐步展开，首先每课是帮助学习者熟悉已有的商务情景和信息的训练，如跟读、分角色朗读等。其次进入角色扮演的训练，是由学习者在学完课文的内容后编排出相关的商务情景，进行商务情景会话的操练，学后做，调动学习者自身的语言能力来实战演练。练习的内容上，突出一些与课文相关的商务技能和商务文化情景的训练和再现。练习的最后是完成任务的训练，设计了任务目标，让学习者在“做中学”，实现教学任务和现实世界的社会经济生活的结合。

三、教学建议

一般的进度，建议每篇课文和课后练习用6～8课时。这样，如果学习者每周有6～8课时学习本教材，一学期可学完一册书。

教材的信息量大，内容分布广，各单元的场景和内容既相互关联又相互独立，学习者可以根据自己的需要、兴趣和学习时间自由选学。练习的设计具有一定的弹性，教学过程中，可根据学习者的实际水平和教学实际安排灵活掌握。

本系列教材的编写得到了中国国家汉办和对外经济贸易大学的领导和专家们的大力支持和帮助，特表谢意。教材中有何不当之处，敬请读者予以指正，以便进一步修订。

对外经济贸易大学　季瑾

2010年4月于惠园

Business Preface

A General Course for Business Chinese（1-3）is a comprehensive course book on business Chinese, aiming to improve the communicative skills of business Chinese learners. The course book suits the needs of those business Chinese learners who have attained a certain level (equivalent to HSK Grade III or above). This series of course books are based on situational scenes, which are convenient for multimedia teaching of business Chinese, and conducive to virtual business Chinese teaching on the Internet platform.

I. The Basic Composition of the Book

A General Course for Business Chinese (1) consists of six units, each of which contains 2 or 3 texts, totaling 13 texts. A General Course for Business Chinese (2) consists of six units, each of which contains 2 texts, totaling 12 texts. A General Course for Business Chinese (3) consists of six units, each of which contains 1 text to 3 texts, totaling 12 texts. Each unit includes text(s), new words, proper nouns, notes and exercises. Each text is matched with Pinyin (Chinese phonetic symbol) and English translation; new words and notes are both bilingual. A corresponding CD-ROM is attached to each copy.

II. The Main Features of the Book

1. The practicality and effectiveness of the thematic materials

The course books cater for business Chinese learners in their business communication activities, emphasizing the combination of special knowledge, working skills and language basics. They are not just simple collections of news items from economic newspapers or journals, but provide systematic, novel and practical communicative skills for our learners from the aspects of language and business.

The grammar in these books serves the learning of business communications; the explanation of grammar helps the learners to remove the language barriers while studying the business content. The grammar in the notes is illuminated with examples and interesting explanations. In addition, the notes also touch upon idioms, popular phrases, knowledge about culture and business.

The exercises in these books consist of language structure training and business communication training. The former is designed for learners to understand and use the Chinese phrases and patterns. The types of exercises are basically fixed and consistent and therefore more systematic. However, with different language points the types of exercises in some texts are accordingly modified.

The business communication training is divided into the four aspects of listening, speaking, reading and writing, and the tasks include reading aloud, reading comprehension, role playing and mission accomplishing.

2. The business content

The content of the course books is focused on the basic knowledge of business communication. The 18 units of the three books are actually 18 topics of business communication, each of which contains 2-3 aspects of the topic. The content forms a connected whole through different situations so as to enlarge the volume of business information, to enhance the learners' memory of relevant knowledge, and to establish an information platform for business Chinese learners.

In the process of learning business knowledge, both social exchanges and hot topics are included, such as business tours, reception, negotiations, trade procedures, jobs, corporate management and culture, tendering, agency, market research, marketing and advertising, investment, trademark law, intellectual property, Canton fair, financing etc.

Required by business communication, we have also added some real business charts, contracts, L/C letters, resumes, advertisements, tendering procedures, agency agreement and questionnaires.

3. The communicative and task-oriented arrangement of format and exercises

The texts are arranged along the story line of several major business people participating in business activities. The business knowledge is learned through situational conversations and business Chinese practiced in real business communication occasions.

The focus of the exercises is in the training of business content which unfolds through different stages. The first is to help the learners to familiarize themselves with the specific business situation through shadow reading and reading aloud. Second, the learners may do role playing by making up their own conversations based on the text, which may very well stimulate their potentials in learning Chinese. In the content of the exercises, business skills related to the text and the reproduction of business situations are especially highlighted. The ultimate objective of the exercises is to help learners to learn by doing, thus combining the class teaching with the real practicing of our social and economic life.

III. Suggestions for the teaching

The average pace of the class is advised to be set at 6-8 class hours for each text including exercises. Thus learners may finish the studying of book (1), book (2) or book (3) in a semester if they spend 6-8 class hours every week.

This series of course books are rather extensive and diverse in their contents, and the situations of the units are both connected and relatively independent, so the learners may choose and learn conveniently according to their needs, interests and time. The design of the exercises is flexible. The teachers may have the liberty to arrange their own classes according to the actual level of the learners.

I hereby extend my heartfelt gratitude to the leaders and experts from Hanban and UIBE for their great support and assistance in the compilation of the course books. All comments from the readers are welcome and will be used for reference to further revision of these books.

Ji Jin
April 2010
UIBE

主要人物介绍
Introduction to the main characters

马莉——女，意大利人（Maria Luigi），意大利爱玛服装公司中国分公司的总经理

Maria Luigi——female, from Italy; general manager of Italian Emma (China) Garment Co. Ltd.

比尔——男，美国人（Bill Andrew），原来是职业经理人，辞职后在对外经济贸易大学中国经济贸易实务研修班进修

Bill Andrew——male, from the US; formerly a professional manager, now studying in the Graduate Program for Chinese Economic and Trade Practice of UIBE

赵红——女，中国人，对外经济贸易大学国际贸易专业四年级的学生

Zhao Hong——female, from China; a senior student majoring in International Trade at UIBE

齐远——男，中国人，对外经济贸易大学MBA二年级的学生

Qi Yuan——male, from China; in his second year of UIBE's MBA Program

马莉和比尔是老朋友。齐远和赵红是比尔在对外经济贸易大学认识的朋友。马莉希望利用业余时间提高自己的商务汉语水平，比尔介绍齐远和赵红辅导马莉。他们四个人成了好朋友。

Maria and Bill are old friends. Bill gets acquainted with Qi Yuan and Zhao Hong at UIBE. Maria wishes to improve her level of business Chinese in her spare time and Bill introduces Qi Yuan and Zhao Hong to help Maria with her Chinese. The four become good friends.

目　录

BUSINESS

Contents

第一单元

Unit 1

Gōngsī guǎnlǐ

公司管理

Corporate Management

课文一

Gōngsī zhèngzài jìnxíng zǔzhī jiégòu de tiáozhěng

公司正在进行组织结构的调整

Qí Yuǎn、Mǎ Lì、Bǐ'ěr zài Duìwài Jīngjì Màoyì Dàxué fùjìn de kāfēiguǎn lǐ liáotiān.

齐远、马莉、比尔在对外经济贸易大学附近的咖啡馆里聊天。

Bǐ'ěr: MǎLì, zhè jǐ tiān máng shénme ne?
比 尔：马莉，这几天忙什么呢？

Mǎ Lì: Wǒmen gōngsī gāng bìnggòu le liǎngjiā gōngsī, xiànzài zhèngzài jìnxíng zǔzhī jiégòu de tiáozhěng.
马 莉：我们公司刚**并购**了两家公司，现在正在进行组织结构的调整。

Bǐ'ěr: Bèi bìnggòu de zhè liǎngjiā gōngsī de yèwù hé nǐmen gōngsī de yíyàng ma?
比 尔：**被并购的这两家公司的业务和你们公司的一样吗**？

Mǎ Lì: Bù yíyàng.Wǒ xiànzài jì yào jǐnkuài shúxī zhè liǎngjiā gōngsī de yèwù qíngkuàng, yòu yào zhěnghé jǐjiā gōngsī de shìchǎng zīyuán, hébìng chóngzǔ xīn de shìchǎng bù.
马 莉：不一样。我现在既要尽快熟悉这两家公司的业务情况，又要**整合**几家公司的市场**资源**，**合并重组**新的市场部。

Qí Yuǎn: Nà nǐ zuìjìn tǐng máng de ba?
齐 远：那你最近挺忙的吧？

Mǎ Lì: Shì ya, wǒ xiànzài yālì hěn dà.
马 莉：是呀，我现在压力很大。

Qí Yuǎn: Bǐ'ěr, nǐ de gōngzuò yālì dà bú dà?
齐 远：比尔，你的工作压力大不大？

Bǐ'ěr: Yě hěn dà. Wǒmen gōngsī yě gānggāng jìnxíng le zǔzhī jiégòu de gǎigé, jiǎnshǎo le yìxiē juécè huánjié.
比 尔：也很大。我们公司也刚刚进行了组织结构的**改革**，**减少**了一些**决策环节**。

Qí Yuǎn: Shì ma? Nǐde gōngzuò yǒu shénme biànhuà ma?
齐 远：是吗？你的工作有什么变化吗？

Bǐ'ěr: Yǒu, yǐqián wǒ dōu shì xiàng bùmén jīnglǐ huìbào gōngzuò, xiànzài bùmén jīnglǐ bèi qǔxiāo le, wǒ zhíjiē xiàng gōngsī de fù zǒngjīnglǐ huìbào gōngzuò.
比 尔：有，以前我都是向**部门**经理**汇报**工作，现在部门经理被**取消**了，我直接向公司的**副**总经理汇报工作。

Mǎ Lì: Nǐmen gōngsī de gōngzuò xiàolǜ yīnggāi tígāo le hěn duō ba?

马　莉：你们公司的工作效率应该提高了很多吧？

Bǐ'ěr: Méi cuòr, gōngsī de juécè bǐ yǐqián kuài le hěn duō, gōngzuò xiàolǜ tígāo le. Dànshì wǒ chéngdān de zérèn gèng zhòng le, yālì yě dà.

比　尔：没错儿，公司的决策比以前快了很多，工作效率提高了。但是我**承担**的**责任**更重了，压力也大。

Mǎ Lì: Qí Yuǎn, nǐ de xīn gōngsī zěnmeyàng?

马　莉：齐远，你的新公司怎么样？

Qí Yuǎn: Wǒmen gōngsī hěn dà, yǒu hěn duō chǎnpǐn shìyèbù, měigè chǎnpǐn shìyèbù dōu yǒu zìjǐ dúlì de yánfābù、shēngchǎnbù hé xiāoshòubù, yǒu dúlì de chǎnpǐn yèwù liúchéng.

齐　远：我们公司很大，有很多产品**事业部**，每个产品事业部都有自己**独立**的**研发**部、生产部和销售部，有独立的产品业务**流程**。

Bǐ'ěr: Nǐ jùtǐ zuò shénme?

比　尔：你具体做什么？

Qí Yuǎn: Wǒ xūyào xiángxì liǎojiě wǒmen shìyèbù xiāoshòu de chǎnpǐn, búduàn de kāifā xīn de shìchǎng zīyuán, xúnzhǎo xīn de kèhù. Wǒ yě miànlín zhe hěn dà de tiǎozhàn.

齐　远：我需要详细了解我们事业部销售的产品，不断地**开发**新的市场资源，寻找新的客户。我也面临着很大的挑战。

Bǐ'ěr: Kànlái wǒmen dōu yíyàng!

比　尔：看来我们都一样！

Text 1

The company is undergoing organizational restructuring

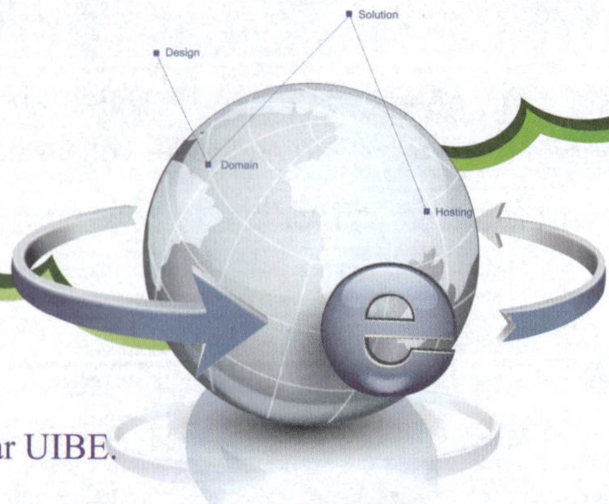

Qi Yuan,Maria, and Bill are chatting in a café near UIBE.

Bill: Maria, what have you been doing these days?

Maria: Our company has just taken over two companies, and now we are conducting organizational restructuring.

Bill: Are these two acquired companies in the same line of business as your company?

Maria: Not the same. Now I have to familiarize myself with the business operations of the two companies as soon as possible; at the same time I have to integrate their market resources and merge them into a new marketing department.

Qi Yuan: Then you must be very busy these days?

Maria: Yes, I'm under a lot of pressure.

Qi Yuan: Bill, do you have any pressure from your job?

Bill: Yes, I have. Our company has just undergone an organizational reform and reduced a few decision-making procedures.

Qi Yuan: Really? Are there any changes in your work?

Bill: Yes, I reported to departmental manager before, and now the position of departmental manager has been cancelled, and I report directly to vice general manager.

Maria: The efficiency of your company must have improved a lot, right?

Bill: That's right, the decision making of the company becomes much faster, and the efficiency has been improved. But my responsibility is bigger; the pressure is heavier as well.

Maria: Qi Yuan, what about your new company?

Qi Yuan: Our company is very big with many product divisions; and each division has independent departments for research and development, production and sales; each has an independent business process for its products.

Bill: What do you do specifically?

Qi Yuan: I need to know the details of those products sold by our division, develop new market resources and look for new customers. I'm also faced with big challenges.

Bill: It looks as if we have the same story!

生词 New words

1	进行	jìnxíng	conduct
2	组织	zǔzhī	organization
3	结构	jiégòu	structure
4	调整	tiáozhěng	to adjust
5	并购	bìnggòu	take over; M&A(merger and acquisition)
6	整合	zhěnghé	to integrate
7	资源	zīyuán	resources
8	合并	hébìng	to merge
9	重组	chóngzǔ	to reorganize
10	改革	gǎigé	to reform; reformation
11	减少	jiǎnshǎo	to decrease; to reduce
12	决策	juécè	strategic decision; make a strategic decision
13	环节	huánjié	procedure
14	部门	bùmén	department
15	汇报	huìbào	to report
16	取消	qǔxiāo	to cancel
17	副	fù	(in job titles) deputy or assistant
18	承担	chéngdān	to undertake; to assume
19	责任	zérèn	responsibility
20	事业部	shìyèbù	division department
21	独立	dúlì	independently

22	研发	yánfā	research and development
23	流程	liúchéng	procedures; flow
24	开发	kāifā	to develop; open up

注释 Notes

1．我们公司刚并购了两家公司，现在正在进行组织结构的调整。

Our company has just taken over two companies and now we are conducting organizational restructuring.

"进行"，动词，"进行＋宾语"表示从事持续性的活动，宾语代表所从事的活动，"进行"后面可以带"了"，一般不带"着、过"。"进行"后面的宾语常常是动词。使用"进行"时应该注意下面几点：

"进行"， a verb; "进行＋ object" refers to a continuous action, the object referring to the action. "进行" may be followed with "了", usually not with "着、过". The object following "进行" is often a verb. The following points should be paid attention to when using "进行":

（1）代表所从事活动的词不能是单音节的。例如：

The word referring to the action should not be a single syllable. For example:

错误的 incorrect	进行查	进行比	进行谈
正确的 correct	进行调查	进行比较	进行谈判

（2）当宾语是动词时，动词不能再带宾语。如果必须得加一个动作的受事，表受事的名词可用介词"对"引进。例如：

When the object is a verb, the verb can not introduce an object. If an recipient must be added to the verb, the noun representing the recipient might be introduced by "对". For example:

主语 subject	对	受事 recipient	进行	动词宾语 object
我们	对	这个问题	进行了	讨论
双方		价格		谈判
他们		市场情况		调查

（3）只用于比较正式、严肃的活动，不用于短暂性的或日常生活中的活动。例如："进行午睡"、"进行叫喊"、"进行说话" 是不可以的。

It can only be used in formal or solemn actions, not used in temporary or dailyactivities. For example, " 进行午睡 ", " 进行叫喊 ", " 进行说话 " are not appropriate.

2. 被并购的这两家公司的业务和你们公司的一样吗？

Are these two acquired companies in the same line of business with your company?

"被字句"的格式一般是"受事＋被＋施事＋动词＋其他"，当我们知道"施事"是谁或"施事"没必要说时，"施事"可以省略不说，例如：

The pattern of "被字句" is usually "recipient＋被＋actor＋verb＋other"， for example:

受事 recipient	被	（施事）(actor)	动词 verb	其他 other
她的手机	被	（小偷）	偷	走了。
行李		（水）	冲	走了。

"被＋(施事)＋动词＋的"可以放在"受事"的前面做定语。例如：路边停着一辆被撞坏的车。

"被＋(actor)＋verb＋的" may be put before "recipient" as an attributive. For example: Along the side of the road parked a wrecked car.

3. 我现在既要尽快熟悉这两家公司的业务情况，又要整合几家公司的市场资源，合并重组新的市场部。

Now I have to familiarize myself with the business operations of the two companies as soon as possible; at the same time I have to integrate their market resources and merge them into a new marketing department.

"尽+～"表示努力达到最大限度，常用的词语有"尽早、尽快、尽量"。例如：

"尽+～" means to exert the utmost efforts, common phrases including "尽早、尽快、尽量". For example:

（1）发现了问题要**尽早**向副总经理汇报。

Report your findings to the vice general manager as soon as possible.

（2）请贵方**尽快**准备好合同文本。

Please prepare your contract as soon as possible.

（3）面试的时候应**尽量**避免谈待遇的问题。

Try to avoid mentioning the issue of salary during an interview.

4. 以前我都是向部门经理汇报工作。

I reported to departmental manager before.

"向"介词，引进动作的对象，跟名词、代词组合，只用在动词前，如果句中有助动词，助动词要放在"向"的前面。例如：

"向" is a preposition, introducing an object of an action; combined with noun or pronoun, it is used before the verb; an auxiliary that appears in the sentence should be put before "向". For example:

主语 subject	谓语 predicate			
	助动词 auxiliary	向	动作的对象 Recipient of action	动词/动宾结构 verb/ verb-object structure
我们	应该	向	跨国公司	学习。
她	——		老师	借了一本书。
我	得		副总经理	汇报工作。

课文二

Tā de guǎnlǐ lǐniàn fēicháng xiānjìn

他的管理理念非常先进

Zhōumò, Zhào Hóng、Qí Yuǎn hé Bǐ' ěr zài Àolínpǐkè gōngyuán lǐ biān zǒu biān liáo.

周末，赵红、齐远和比尔在奥林匹克公园里边走边聊。

Qí Yuǎn: Zhào Hóng, zuìjìn xuéxí máng ma?

齐　远：赵红，最近学习忙吗？

Zhào Hóng: Kè dōu shàng wán le, wǒ xiànzài zài yì jiā qìchē gōngsī shíxí.
赵　红：课都上完了，我现在在一家汽车公司实习。

Qí Yuǎn: Gōngsī hái kěyǐ ba?
齐　远：公司还可以吧？

Zhào Hóng: Hái kěyǐ, gōngsī de guīmó bú tài dà.
赵　红：还可以，公司的**规模**不太大。

Bǐ'ěr: Shì zuò nǐ yǐqián shuō de shìchǎng diàoyán gōngzuò ma?
比　尔：是做你以前说的**市场调研**工作吗？

Zhào Hóng: Búshì, wǒ xiànzài cānyù gōngsī chǎnpǐn de yíngxiāo cèhuà gōngzuò, zhè yě shì wǒ mèngmèiyǐqiú de.
赵　红：不是，我现在参与公司产品的营销**策划**工作，这也是我**梦寐以求**的。

Bǐ'ěr: Néng zuò zìjǐ xǐhuan de shìr, zhè tǐng nándé de.
比　尔：能做自己喜欢的事儿，这挺**难得**的。

Qí Yuǎn: Nǐmen gōngsī duì xīn yuángōng jìnxíng péixùn ma?
齐　远：你们公司对新员工进行**培训**吗？

Zhào Hóng: Dāngrán le. Yuángōng gāng jìn gōngsī hé bèi tíshēng de shíhòu, gōngsī dōu yào duì tāmen jìnxíng péixùn.
赵　红：当然了。员工刚进公司和被**提升**的时候，公司都要对他们进行培训。

Qí Yuǎn: Hái yǒu nǎxiē huódòng?
齐　远：还有哪些活动？

Zhào Hóng: Gōngsī hái huì bú dìngqī de zǔzhī yuángōng cānjiā tuòzhǎn xùnliàn, péiyǎng yuángōng de tuánduì hézuò yìshí.
赵　红：公司还会**不定期**地组织员工参加**拓展训练**，**培养**员工的**团队合作意识**。

Bǐ'ěr: Nǐmen de lǎobǎn zěnmeyàng?
比　尔：你们的老板怎么样？

Zhào Hóng: Wǒ fēicháng xīnshǎng xiànzài de lǎobǎn. Wǒ juéde tā de guǎnlǐ lǐniàn fēicháng xiānjìn, guǎnlǐ fāngfǎ yě hěn yǒuxiào.
赵　红：我非常**欣赏**现在的老板。我觉得他的管理理念非常先进，管理方法也很有效。

Qí Yuǎn: Lǎobǎn de guǎnlǐ fāngfǎ hé guǎnlǐ nénglì juédìng zhe gōngsī de fāzhǎn fāngxiàng.
齐　远：老板的管理方法和管理能力决定着公司的发展方向。

Zhào Hóng: Kě bú shì ma, tīngshuō, wǒmen gōngsī liǎngnián yǐqián chàdiǎnr pòchǎn le. Xiànzài de lǎobǎn shōugòu zhègè gōngsī yǐhòu, jìnxíng le quánmiàn gǎigé. Xiànzài wǒmen gōngsī měi gè yuè de xiāoshòu liàng hé xiāoshòu lìrùn dōu zài búduàn zēngjiā.
赵　红：可不是嘛，听说，我们公司两年以前差点儿**破产**了。现在的老板**收购**这个公司以后，进行了**全面**改革。现在我们公司每个月的**销售量**和销售**利润**都在**不断增加**。

Bǐ'ěr: Kànlái nǐ duì nǐ xiànzài de gōngsī fēicháng mǎnyì.
比　尔：看来你对你现在的公司非常满意。

Zhào Hóng: Shì a. Gōngsī hěn zhòngshì yuángōng qiánlì de kāifā. Wǒ juéde zài zhègè gōngsī gōngzuò, zìjǐ de nénglì kěyǐ dédào hěn hǎo de fāhuī.
赵　红：是啊。公司很**重视**员工**潜力**的开发。我觉得在这个公司工作，自己的能力可以得到很好的**发挥**。

Bǐ'ěr: Nǐmen gōngsī zhème hǎo, wǒ gāncuì tiàocáo qù nǐmen gōngsī ba.
比　尔：你们公司这么好，我**干脆跳槽**去你们公司吧。

Zhào Hóng: Dé le ba, nǐmen gōngsī duō hǎo ya! Gōngzuò fēnwéi nàme hǎo, gěi yuángōng tígōng de fāzhǎn jīhuì yòu duō.
赵　红：得了吧，你们公司多好呀！工作**氛围**那么好，给员工提供的发展机会又多。

Qí Yuǎn: Tā zài kāi wánxiào ne, tā nǎ shěde cí qù xiànzài de gōngzuò ya! Lǎobǎn jiù yào tíshēng tā dāng zǒngcái zhùlǐ le.
齐　远：他在开玩笑呢，他哪**舍得**辞去现在的工作呀！老板就要提升他当**总裁**助理了。

Zhào Hóng: Zhēn de ma, Bǐ'ěr? Nǐ děi qǐngkè ya!
赵　红：真的吗，比尔？你得请客呀！

Bǐ'ěr: Hǎo, méi wèntí!
比　尔：好，没问题！

Text 2

His management ideas are very advanced

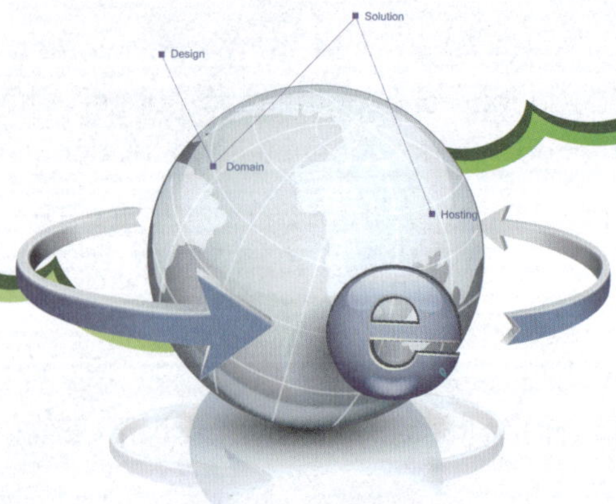

During the weekend, Zhao Hong, Qi Yuan and Bill are walking and talking in the Olympic Park.

Qi Yuan: Zhao Hong, have you been busy in your studies recently?

Zhao Hong: I have finished all my courses and now I'm working as an intern in an auto company.

Qi Yuan: How is the company?

Zhao Hong: It's all right. It's not a big company.

Bill: Are you doing the market research you mentioned earlier?

Zhao Hong: No, now I'm participating in the marketing planning for the company's products, and that's what I dreamed for before.

Bill: You can do things you really like; that's really nice.

Qi Yuan: Does your company have a training program for new employees?

Zhao Hong: Of course. When employees first enter the company or when they get promoted, the company will provide training for them.

Qi Yuan: Are there any other activities?

Zhao Hong: The company will also organize the employees to participate in outward development programs for cultivating a better teamwork spirit.

Bill: How is your boss?

Zhao Hong: I really appreciate my boss. I think his management ideas are very advanced and his managing skills very effective.

Qi Yuan: The management skills and capabilities of a boss help determine the development trend of his company.

Zhao Hong: That's true. I heard our company almost went bankrupt two years ago. The current boss bought this company and undertook a complete overhaul. Now our company's monthly sales and profits are both on the rise.

Bill: You seem to be very satisfied with the company.

Zhao Hong: Yes. Our company attaches great importance to the development of its employees' potentials, so I can bring my capabilities into full play.

Bill: Your company sounds so good. Why don't I simply go work at your company?

Zhao Hong: Are you kidding? What a big company you are working for! Such a fine working environment and so many development opportunities for employees.

Qi Yuan: He was just joking. How could he be willing to resign from such a good job! His boss will soon promote him to the position of president assistant.

Bill: Is that true, Bill? You have to invite us to dinner for that!

Bill: OK, no problem!

生词 New words

1	实习	shíxí	intern
2	规模	guīmó	scale; scope; extent
3	市场调研	shìchǎng diàoyán	market research
4	策划	cèhuà	to plan; to plot; to scheme
5	梦寐以求	mèngmèiyǐqiú	yearn for something day and night
6	难得	nándé	hard or not possible to come by
7	培训	péixùn	to train;training
8	提升	tíshēng	to promote
9	不定期	bú dìngqī	unscheduled
10	拓展训练	tuòzhǎn xùnliàn	outward development program
11	培养	péiyǎng	to cultivate
12	团队合作	tuánduì hézuò	teamwork
13	意识	yìshí	consciousness
14	欣赏	xīnshǎng	to appreciate
15	破产	pòchǎn	go bankrupt

16	收购	shōugòu	to purchase; acquisition
17	全面	quánmiàn	comprehensive
18	销售量	xiāoshòu liàng	sales volume
19	利润	lìrùn	profits
20	不断	búduàn	uninterrupted; unceasing
21	增加	zēngjiā	to raise; to increase
22	重视	zhòngshì	attach importance to
23	潜力	qiánlì	potential
24	发挥	fāhuī	to bring into play
25	干脆	gāncuì	simply; just; altogether
26	跳槽	tiàocáo	abandon one occupation in favor of another
27	氛围	fēnwéi	atmosphere
28	舍得	shěde	be willing to part with (sth.)
29	总裁	zǒngcái	president

注释 Notes

1. 可不是嘛，听说，我们公司两年以前差点儿破产了，……

That's true. I heard our company almost went bankrupt two years ago.

“可不是”表示同意对方的话，也可以用“可不”。例如：“可不是”is used to express agreement to the other speaker, “可不”may also be used. For example:

（1）A：公司现在的这种组织结构非常不利于公司的发展。

The current organization of the company is detrimental to the development of the company.

B：可不是，早就应该进行改革了。

That's true. We should have reformed it long ago.

（2）A：一定要找一份自己喜欢的工作。

One must find a job he likes.

B：可不，这样工作的时候才开心。

Right, so you can be happy when you work.

2. 我们公司两年以前差点儿破产了。

Our company almost went bankrupt two years ago.

“差点儿”表示某种事情几乎实现却没有实现，或者是几乎不能实现而终于实现了。

“差点儿” indicates that something almost takes place, but does not really happen, or an almost impossible thing is finally realized.

（1）表示不希望实现的事情几乎实现，但结果是没有实现，有庆幸的意思。动词用肯定式或否定式都可以，意思一样。例如：

Indicating something, which you don't expect to happen, nearly takes place. It expresses a tone of being lucky. The affirmative or negative pattern of the verb means the same. For example:

我差点儿（没）摔倒。（事实是没有摔倒）

I almost fell to the ground. (The truth is I didn't fall.)

（2）表示希望实现的事情几乎不能实现，但结果却实现了，有庆幸的意思。动词用否定式。例如：

Indicating something, which you want to happen, nearly didn't happen, and the result is that it really happens. It also expresses a lucky tone. The negative pattern of the verb is used. For example:

那天我差点儿没赶上火车。（事实是赶上火车了）

That day I nearly didn't catch the train. (The truth is I did.)

这次考试我差点儿没及格。（事实是及格了）

I nearly failed in the exam this time. (The truth is I didn't.)

（3）表示希望实现的事情几乎能实现，但结果是没有实现，有可惜的意思。动词用肯定式。例如：

Indicating something, which you wish to happen, nearly happens, but the result is that it doesn't happen. It expresses a feeling of regret. For example:

他差点儿就考上重点大学了。（事实是没考上重点大学）

He was almost admitted by a major university. (The fact is he wasn't.)

他差点儿就被那家公司录用了。（事实是没有被那家公司录用）

He was almost recruited by that company. (The fact is he was not.)

3. 你们公司这么好，我干脆跳槽去你们公司吧。

Your company sounds so good. Why don't I simply go work at your company?

“干脆”，副词，放在动词的前面，表示直截了当，爽快。例如：

“干脆”, an adverb, put before a verb, indicating “straightforward”, “being direct”. For example:

（1）你在那个公司干得那么不开心，干脆辞职算了。

If it makes you so unhappy to work in that company, why don't you just quit?

（2）就一站路，我们干脆步行过去吧，别坐出租车了。

It's only one stop ahead, why don't we just walk there? Let's not take the taxi.

（3）这家公司的报价这么高，我们干脆找别的公司吧。

This company's quoted price is so high, why don't we find another one?

4. 得了吧，你们公司多好呀！

Don't be kidding. What a great company you have there!

“得了”在这里表示否定别人的说法，有不同意的意思，后面常常加“吧”。例如：

“得了” here indicates a negation to others' opinion or a disagreement, usually followed with “吧”. For example:

（1）A: 要是找不到工作，咱们就开一个自己的公司，怎么样？

What do you think opening a company of our own if we can't find a job?

B: 得了吧，我们现在哪有钱开公司呀？

Don't be kidding. Where do we find enough money to open a company?

（2）A: 如果让我管理公司，我一定能把公司管理得非常好。

If I'm allowed to manage the company, I'll be sure manage it pretty well.

B: 得了吧，你连自己的事情都管不好，还管理公司呢！

Don't be kidding. You can't even manage your own things not to mention a company.

5. 他哪舍得辞去现在的工作呀！

How could he be willing to resign from such a good job!

这是一个反问句，意思是“他不舍得辞去现在的工作”。“哪”用在动词前面，表示否定。例如：

This is a rhetorical question, meaning “he is not willing to resign from his job.” “ 哪 ”is used before the verb, indicating a negation. For example:

（1）我不信，哪有这样的事。
I don’t believe it, how could there be such a thing?

（2）我现在工作忙得不得了，哪有时间陪你去逛街呀。
I’m really too busy working. How could I have time to go window-shopping with you?

（3）他哪舍得把他的新房子租给别人。
How could he be willing to rent his new house to others?

练习
Exercises

一、跟读生词并且纠音。
Read the new words after the teacher and correct your pronunciation.

二、跟读课文并且纠音。
Read the texts after the teacher and correct your pronunciation.

三、学生分组，分角色朗读课文一、二。
Divide the students into groups and read the texts 1 & 2 in different roles.

四、学生分组，不看书分角色表演课文一、二。
Divide the students into groups and role play the texts 1 & 2 without referring to the book.

五、角色扮演。
Role play.

几个人一组，分为不同的角色来对话，讨论一些和公司有关的问题。请注意使用课文中的词语和句子来表达。

提示和要求：

（一）请根据下面的问题进行讨论。

1．这个公司的组织结构是什么样的？这种组织结构有哪些优点和缺点？

2．你觉得这个公司需要改革吗？为什么？

3．这个公司对员工进行培训吗？什么时候对员工进行培训？

4．你觉得这个公司的老板怎么样？他的管理理念和管理方法好吗？为什么？

5．这个公司的工作氛围怎么样？

6．你觉得在这个公司工作的员工，他的能力能得到很好的发挥吗？为什么？

（二）注意每个角色的谈话内容不要重复。
（三）可以谈你工作过的公司或现在工作的公司，也可以谈你知道的公司。

六、替换练习。
Substitution drills.

1. <u>公司</u> + 正在进行 + <u>组织结构</u> + 的 + <u>调整</u>。

我们公司	事业部	重组
中国	教育体制	改革
中国	产业结构	调整

2. <u>以前我都是</u> + 向 + <u>部门经理</u> + <u>汇报</u> + <u>工作</u>。

我们要	跨国公司	学习	先进的管理理念
买方	卖方	提出	索赔
他	小王	借了	一本书

3. <u>公司的决策</u> + 比 + <u>以前</u> + <u>快</u> + 了 + 很多。

你的汉语水平	两年前	提高
今天的气温	昨天的	低
我们的价格	其他公司的	便宜
我们公司的效率	去年	高

4. <u>你们公司</u> + 对 + <u>新员工</u> + 进行 + <u>培训吗</u>？

今天我们	这个问题	讨论
明天双方	付款方式	谈判
公司	新的市场部	重组

5. <u>你们公司这么好</u>，<u>我</u> + 干脆 + <u>跳槽去你们公司</u> + 吧。

这么近，	我们	步行去
最近老吵架，	我们俩	分手
大多数客户在北京	你们公司	搬到北京来

6. <u>他</u> + 哪 + <u>舍得辞去现在的工作</u> + 呀！

我们公司	重视开发员工的潜力
我们的工作效率	提高了
我	熟悉欧洲的市场情况
咱们	吃得了这么多菜

七、把下面的每组词语组成句子。
Make a sentence with the following words in each group.

课文一：

1. 的 公司 被 和 业务 家 公司 的 一样 你们 吗 并购 的 这 两
2. 公司 我 尽快 要 熟悉 业务 这 的 情况 家
3. 公司 的 多 决策 快 以前 比 了 很
4. 我 的 更 承担 了 责任 重
5. 个 研发部 销售部 产品事业部 生产部 都 自己 有 独立 的 和 每
6. 不断 需要 新 开发 地 市场 的 我 资源
7. 的 也 挑战 面临 很大 着 我

课文二：

1. 你 是 调研 的 做 市场 说 吗 工作 以前
2. 公司 组织 还 会 参加 不定期地 拓展训练 员工
3. 我 的 先进 觉得 管理 他 非常 理念
4. 公司的 老板的 管理 着 管理 发展 决定 和 方法 能力 方向
5. 破产 我们 以前 公司 两年 差点儿 了
6. 我们 不断 公司 个 销售利润 增加 销售量 月 在 都 和 每 的

7. 公司　潜力　开发　很　员工　重视　的

8. 老板　就要　了　总裁　他　提升　当　助理

八、请把下面的动词和它的宾语用线连起来。

Please link the following verbs with their objects.

	动词	宾语
1.	调整	市场资源
	整合	组织结构
	减少	新的市场
	培训	决策环节
	开发	部门经理
	参加	合作意识
	培养	拓展训练
2.	开发	效率
	发挥	挑战
	提高	责任
	面临	潜力
	承担	作用

九、选词填空。

Choose the words given below to fill in the blanks.

汇报　减少　调整　承担　开发　决策　并购　取消　干脆　面临

1. 我们公司刚被一家法国公司（　　　）了。
2. 你（　　　）辞职来我们公司吧。
3. 从下个月开始，我们公司将进行组织结构的（　　　）。
4. 职位高的人（　　　）的责任也大。
5. 公司的重大（　　　）都是由董事会作出的。
6. 我应该向人力资源部经理（　　　）工作。
7. 只有不断地（　　　）新的产品，才能满足市场的需求。
8. 由于天气的原因，今天下午飞往香港的航班（　　　）了。

9. 我被提升为副总经理以后，(　　　) 着更大的压力和挑战。

10. 他们的产品改为直销以后，(　　　) 了很多中间环节。

十、用所给的词完成对话。

Complete the dialogues with the words in the brackets.

1. A：请问贵方何时能把合同文本寄来？
   B：抱歉！ ________________。(尽快)
2. A：你们公司的市场部也负责策划营销工作吗？
   B：不，________________。(独立)
3. A：赵红现在的工作待遇很好，但压力也不大。
   B：是呀，________________。(难得)
4. A：你觉得营销策略对公司的销售利润有影响吗？
   B：当然，________________。(决定着)
5. A：我们公司再不改革就要破产了。
   B：________________。(可不是吗)
6. A：听说你的辅导老师考上研究生了，是吗？
   B：对呀，不过 ________________。(差点儿)
7. A：我如果每天都来上课，一定能通过 HSK 的 8 级。
   B：________________。(得了吧)

十一、请说一说下面句子的意思。

Please tell the meaning of the following sentences.

1. 昨天早上他差点儿没迟到。
2. 刚下了雨，路面上有很多水，我差点儿摔倒了。
3. 昨天路上堵车，我差点儿就赶不上飞机了。
4. 当年他差点儿就考上北京大学了。
5. 我和我的老朋友十年没见了，我差点儿没认出他来。
6. 这次 HSK 的考试，他差点儿就通过 6 级了。

十二、把下面的句子变成反问句。
Change the following sentences into a rhetorical question.

1. 我不熟悉我们公司在中国北方的业务情况。
2. 他不舍得把他的新房子租给别人。
3. 我还有那么多工作要做，没有时间去看电影。
4. 我不知道这件事。
5. 她现在的工作很好，不愿意辞职。
6. 这件事我们俩都有责任，不能让你一个人承担。

十三、阅读理解。
Reading comprehension.

下面是记者与诺基亚（中国）投资有限公司人力资源部刘经理的一段对话：

问：诺基亚员工是否面临着很大的压力？

刘：不同的人情况不一样。在诺基亚谈压力，主要取决于你怎么看待学习的问题，诺基亚的压力主要是学习的压力，工作的过程就是学习的过程。员工工作时间都比较长，一边工作一边学习确实不是一件容易的事，比正常学习要辛苦得多，但由于你在这个行业，你喜欢这个工作，你就需要适应行业的变化，学习是自然而然的，其实也并没有想象的那么困难。

问：从诺基亚的组织结构来看，管理的层级比较少，这种扁平的管理是否会使员工失去更多的晋升机会和发展空间？

刘：层级少的话，这方面的 Motivation 要低得多。但职务的晋升并不是惟一的激励因素。在职业发展方面我们给员工提供优先机会，一旦有了职位空缺，我们都是先内部宣布，两周后没有结果再向外公布。除此以外，我们还为员工提供各种培训机会，包括很多出国培训及合作做项目的机会，以芬兰为主，瑞士、美国、亚太地区都有，这对员工来讲也是非常具有吸引力的。

问：诺基亚最吸引员工的是什么？

刘：诺基亚最吸引员工的是公司提供给员工的自由度、信任和发展空间。我在这儿工作快 6 年了，我感觉诺基亚是比较宽松的一个公司，自主度比较大。几年间虽然换了 5 个老板，但人都不错，会给员工很多信任和空间，你可以做很多事情。总部的一些人也很 Open。另外，诺基亚变化非常频繁，不断有机会出现，能让员工不断学到新东西。

根据上面的这段对话，判断正误。

1. 诺基亚的员工都面临着很大的压力。（　　）
2. 由于诺基亚的管理层级比较少，这种扁平的管理使员工失去了更多的晋升机会和发展空间。（　　）
3. 有职位空缺的时候，诺基亚常常先提升公司内部的员工。（　　）
4. 诺基亚为员工提供很多出国培训的机会。（　　）
5. 诺基亚给员工提供的发展空间不大。（　　）
6. 在诺基亚，员工能不断地学到新东西。（　　）

十四、复述课文一和课文二。
Retell the texts 1 & 2.

十五、完成任务。
Complete the tasks.

1. **调查并报告：**

（1）没有工作过的同学，请你在网上调查一家公司的组织结构，然后在课堂上向你的老师和同学报告。

（2）工作过的同学，请在课堂上向你的老师和同学报告你们公司的组织结构情况。

2. **请向你工作过的同学或是朋友调查：**了解他或她工作过的公司的福利制度、培训制度、工作气氛等情况。

第二单元

Unit 2

Qǐyè wénhuà

企业文化

Corporate Culture

课文一

Hěnduō wàiqǐ xǐhuan lùyòng běntǔ réncái

很多外企喜欢录用本土人才

Qí Yuǎn、Zhào Hóng、Mǎ Lì、Bǐ'ěr zài kāfēitīng liáotiān.

齐远、赵红、马莉、比尔在咖啡厅聊天。

Zhào Hóng: Mǎlì, tīngshuō nǐ zuìjìn zài zhāopìn xīn yuángōng?
赵　红：马莉，听说你最近在招聘新员工？

Mǎ Lì: Bié tí le! Miànshì le nàme duō yě méiyǒu héshì de, zhēn ràng wǒ tóuténg.
马　莉：别提了！面试了那么多也没有合适的，真让我**头疼**。

Qí Yuǎn: Nǐ kěyǐ bǎ zhèxiē gōngzuò wàibāo gěi zhōngguó běntǔ zhuānyè de rénlì zīyuán gōngsī a.
齐　远：你可以把这些工作**外包**给中国本土专业的人力资源公司啊。

Bǐ'ěr: Qí Yuǎn shuō de méi cuò,hěn duō zài zhōngguó de wàiqǐ shì zhème zuò de.Zhèyàng jì néng jiàngdī gōngsī de chéngběn, yòu kěyǐ bǐjiào kuài de zhāopìn dào yèwù nénglì qiáng de réncái.
比　尔：齐远说得没错，很多在中国的外企是这么做的。这样既能降低公司的成本，又可以比较快地招聘到业务能力强的人才。

Zhào Hóng: Hěn duō wàiqǐ xǐhuan lùyòng běntǔ réncái, hái yīnwéi běntǔ réncái shúxī dāngdì de shìchǎng hé fēngtǔ rénqíng.
赵　红：很多外企喜欢录用本土人才，还因为本土人才熟悉当地的市场和**风土人情**。

Qí Yuǎn: Nǐ shuō de méi cuò, bǐrú shuō Mótuōluólā de zhōngguó yuángōng jiù yǐjīng dádào yí wàn rén, jīnglǐ rényuán de běntǔhuà bǐlì yě gāo dá 80%.
齐　远：你说得没错，比如说**摩托罗拉**的中国员工就已经达到1万人，经理人员的**本土化**比例也高**达**80%。

Bǐ'ěr: Shuōdào "běntǔhuà ", wǒmen diànnǎo hángyè, Huìpǔ gōngsī de běntǔhuà jīngyíng jiù zuò de bú cuò.
比　尔：说到"本土化"，我们电脑行业，**惠普**公司的本土化经营就做得不错。

Zhào Hóng: Ó, tāmen shì zěnme zuòde?
赵　红：哦，他们是怎么做的？

Bǐ' ěr: Jìnrù zhōngguó hòu, tāmen de xiāoshòu zuò le yìxiē gǎijìn, bǐrú zēngjiā le èr jí jīngxiāo hé fēnxiāo, wèi gùkè tígōng le gèng fāngbiàn de fúwù.
比　尔：进入中国后，他们的销售作了一些**改进**，比如增加了二级**经销**和**分销**，为顾客提供了更方便的服务。

Qí Yuǎn: Kěndéjī zuò de yě hěn chénggōng.Tāmen zǒng néng búduàn de tuīchū shìhé zhōngguó rén kǒuwèi de xīn pǐnzhǒng.
齐　远：**肯德基**做得也很成功。他们总能不断地**推出**适合中国人**口味**的新**品种**。

Zhào Hóng: Nǐ jiù zhīdào chī!
赵　红：你就知道吃！

Mǎ Lì: Wǎnshang wǒmen qù chī Běijīng kǎoyā ba! Zhè kěshì Běijīng zuì běntǔ de!
马　莉：晚上我们去吃北京烤鸭吧！这可是北京最本土的！

Text 1

Many foreign enterprises prefer local talents

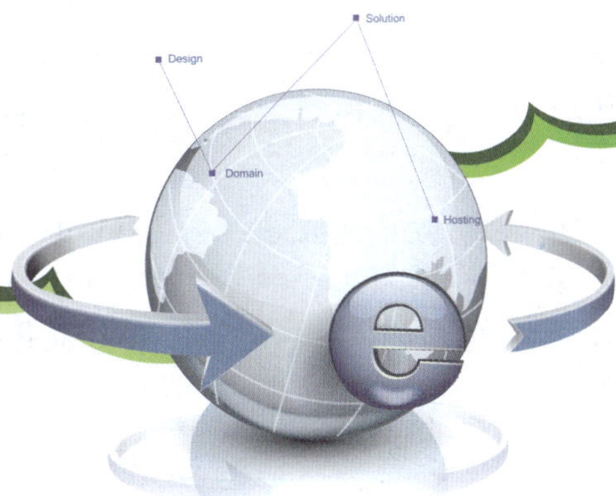

Qi Yuan, Zhao Hong, Maria and Bill are chatting in a café.

Zhao Hong: Maria, I have heard you're recruiting new employees?

Maria: Don't mention it! I have interviewed so many, but no one is suitable. It really gives me headaches.

Qi Yuan: You may outsource to a professional human resources company here in China.

Bill: Qi Yuan is right. Many foreign enterprises in China do that. In this way they can reduce cost and are able to hire competent personnel.

Zhao Hong: Many foreign firms like to hire local talent, because local people are familiar with the local markets and customs.

Qi Yuan: You're right. For instance, the Chinese personnel of Motorola now number 10,000 and its local managers account for 80% of the total.

Bill: Speaking of "localization", the computer company HP has done quite well in its localization strategy.

Zhao Hong: Oh, how did they do?

Bill: After they went into China, they improved their sales strategy. For example they added secondary dealing and distribution to provide customers with more convenient services.

Qi Yuan: KFC has been successful as well. They can always come up with new products to fit the Chinese tastes.

Zhao Hong: You know nothing but eating!

Maria: Let's go to have the Beijing Roast Duck tonight! It's a local food here in Beijing.

生词 New words

1	本土	běntǔ	native;local
2	头疼	tóuténg	have a headache
3	外包	wàibāo	to outsource
4	风土人情	fēngtǔrénqíng	local customs and culure
5	本土化	běntǔhuà	localilzation
6	达	dá	to extend,reach
7	改进	gǎijìn	to improve
8	经销	jīngxiāo	to sell
9	分销	fēnxiāo	to distribute
10	推出	tuīchū	to come up with
11	口味	kǒuwèi	taste
12	品种	pǐnzhǒng	variety

专有名词 Proper nouns

1. 摩托罗拉
   Mótuōluólā
   Motorola Inc.
2. 惠普
   Huìpǔ
   HP , Hewlett-Packard Development Company, L.P.
3. 肯德基
   Kěndéjī
   KFC(Kentucky Fried Chicken)

注释 Notes

1. 真让我头疼。

It really gives me headaches.

“头疼”，形容词，头部疼痛。比喻感到为难或者讨厌。例如：

“头疼”, adjective, the head aches. It’s a metaphor for something difficult or loathsome. For example:

（1）一想到每月一次的英文考试，我就头疼。
It gives me headaches to think of the monthly English test.

（2）令我头疼的是，没有合适的礼服参加同事的婚礼。
What gives me headaches is that I don’t have a formal attire for my colleague’s wedding.

（3）杰克喜欢问千奇百怪的问题，常常让老师感到头疼。
Jack likes to ask weird questions, which often gives the teacher headaches.

2. 你说得没错，比如说摩托罗拉的中国员工就已经达到 1 万人。

You’re right. For instance, the Chinese personnel of Motorola number 10,000.

“比如说”，“例如，比如”的意思，表示举例说明。例如：

“比如说”， means “for instance”, “such as”. For example:

（1）北京变化很大，比如说兴建了很多高楼大厦。
Beijing has changed a lot. For example, many skyscrapers have been built.

（2）我游览过不少名胜古迹，比如说故宫、长城、兵马俑。
I .ve toured many famous attractions. For instance, the Forbidden City, the GreatWall and the Terracotta Warriors.

（3）我的老板很体贴员工，比如说给每位员工寄生日卡片。
My boss is very considerate towards the employees. For instance, he sends birthday cards to every employee.

3. 经理人员的本土化比例也高达80%。

Its local managers account for 80% of the total.

本土化，本地化。在经济领域，跨国公司为了适应所在国家独特的文化和风俗习惯，将生产、管理、营销、人事等融入当地的经济过程。他们为了积极适应所在国家或地区的环境和市场，调整或改变原有的经营方法和策略，经营活动要充分考虑当地市场和消费者的心理和习惯，以实现最大程度的盈利。例如：

本土化，localization. In the economic realm, multinational corporations merge their production, management, marketing and human resources into the local economic process in order to suit the unique culture and customs of the country. They adjust or change their original business strategies to fit the local markets and environments. To get the most profits, business operations must be conducted with a view to catering to the local market and the mentality of the local consumers. For example:

（1）这家跨国公司在推进人才本土化时遇到了一些难题。

The multinational company encountered quite a few problems when it pushed for the localization of personnel.

（2）营销本土化是企业成功的一个重要策略。

Marketing localization is an important strategy to the success of an enterprise.

4. 经理人员的本土化比例也高达80%。

Its local managers account for 80% of the total.

"化"是后缀，加在名词或形容词后面构成动词，表示转变成具有某种性质或状态。"名词+化"，比如"全球化、国际化、信息化、产业化、市场化、大众化、个性化、情绪化、汉化"等。"形容词+化"比如"绿化、美化、恶化"等。例如：

"化" is a suffix added to the end of a noun or an adjective, indicating a change into a quality or a state of things. "Noun+化", for example, "全球化、国际化、信息化、产业化、市场化、大众化、个性化、情绪化、汉化" etc. "Adjective+化", for example, "绿化、美化、恶化" etc. For example:

（1）目前，经济全球化的进程加快了。

Now economic globalization has been accelerating.

（2）这些绿色植物美化了环境。

These green plants make the environment more beautiful.

（3）这些产品的设计非常个性化。

The design of these products is full of individuality.

5. 经理人员的本土化比例也高达 80%。

Its local managers account for 80% of the total.

“高达”，表示非常高，达到了……的程度。“形容词 + 达”表示某种状态或性质达到的程度，根据句中话题的需要来搭配不同的形容词，常为单音节词。比如“重达、多达、厚达、长达、宽达”等。例如：

“ 高达 ”, indicates a very high degree, reaching the level of ……“adjective + 达 ” indicates the level a state or quality may reach. Different adjectives, mostly single-character words, may be used to match the needs of a topic, such as “ 重达、多达、厚达、长达、宽达 ”. For example:

（1）这辆跑车的价格高达千万元。

The price of this sports car is ten million yuan.

（2）参加此次运动会的国家多达 135 个。

As many as 135 countries participated in the Games.

（3）这些行李重达 50 公斤，我一个人搬不动。

The luggage weighs 50 kilos and I cannot lift it alone.

6. 说到“本土化”，我们电脑行业，惠普公司的本土化经营就做得不错。

Speaking of “localization”, the computer company HP has done quite well in its localization strategy.

“说到”，是“提到，谈到，谈论到”的意思。例如：

“ 说到” means “mentioning”, “speaking of ”, “talking about”. For example:

（1）说到畅销书，我最喜欢的就是《哈利·波特》。

Speaking of best-sellers, my favorite is *Harry Potter.*

（2）说到成功，人们常常会把它和财富、声望联系起来。

Speaking of success, people usually associate it with fortune and fame.

（3）说到最美丽的地方，我首先想到的就是我的故乡。

Speaking of the most beautiful place, I would first of all think of my hometown.

课文二

Qǐyè wénhuà yě yǒu míngxiǎn de chābié

企业文化也有明显的差别

Bǐ'ěr、Zhào Hóng、Mǎ Lì、Qí Yuǎn zài péngyǒu de wǎnhuì shang biān chī biān liáo.

比尔、赵红、马莉、齐远在朋友的晚会上边吃边聊。

Bǐ'ěr: Wǒ tīngshuō xiànzài hěnduō zhōngguó dàxué bìyèshēng xuǎnzé qù wàiqǐ gōngzuò, wèishénme ne?

比 尔：我听说现在很多中国大学毕业生选择去外企工作，为什么呢？

Mǎ Lì: Zhōngguó de wàiqǐ yuèlái yuèduō bei.（Mǎlì xiào zhe shuō）

马 莉：中国的外企越来越多呗。（马莉笑着说）

Zhào Hóng: Yìbān rén rènwéi,wàiqǐ de yuángōng shōurù gāo,dàiyù hǎo,fāzhǎn kōngjiān dà,hái kěyǐ jiēchù dào xiānjìn de guǎnlǐ wénhuà.

赵 红：一般人认为，外企的员工收入高，待遇好，发展空间大，还可以**接触**到先进的管理文化。

Mǎ Lì: Bù tóng de wàiqǐ,qǐyè wénhuà yě yǒu míngxiǎn de chābié.

马 莉：不同的外企，企业文化也有**明显**的**差别**。

Qí Yuǎn: Méi cuò,wǒ de yī gè péngyǒu zài Rìqǐ gōngzuò,tā de dàiyù fēicháng hǎo, búguò gōngsī de guǎnlǐ hěn yángé,duì shàngsī yào juéduì fúcóng.

齐 远：没错，我的一个朋友在**日企**工作，他的待遇非常好，不过公司的管理很**严格**，对**上司**要**绝对服从**。

Zhào Hóng: Hánzī qǐyè shì bu shì yě zhèyàng?Wǒ yǒu yí gè péngyǒu zài Hánguó gōngsī gōngzuò,tā chángcháng bàoyuàn tāmen jìnshēng de jīhuì bù duō,hái lǎo jiābān.

赵　红：韩资企业是不是也这样？我有一个朋友在**韩国**公司工作，他常常**抱怨**他们**晋升**的机会不多，还**老**加班。

Qí Yuǎn: Mǎ Lì,nà nǐmen Ōuzhōu gōngsī hé Měiguó gōngsī de guǎnlǐ wénhuà yíyàng ma?

齐　远：马莉，那你们欧洲公司和美国公司的管理文化一样吗？

Mǎ Lì: Bù wánquán xiāngtóng ,wǒ juéde Měiguó gōngsī gèng guānxīn shìfǒu yínglì.

马　莉：不完全相同，我觉得美国公司更**关心**是否**盈利**。

Zhào Hóng: Nà Ōuzhōu gōngsī jiù bù zhòngshì gōngsī de lìrùn ma?

赵　红：那欧洲公司就不重视公司的利润吗？

Mǎ Lì: Zhòngshì!Dàn tāmen juéde kèhù de xūqiú hé gōngsī de yínglì tóngyàng zhòngyào.

马　莉：重视！但他们觉得客户的**需求**和公司的盈利同样重要。

Bǐ'ěr: Bùguǎn nǎge guójiā de qǐyè wénhuà dōu shì yǒu tāmen de kěqǔzhīchù de.

比　尔：不管哪个国家的企业文化都是有他们的**可取之处**的。

Zhào Hóng: Suǒyǐ "Shìjiè wǔbǎi qiáng"de páihángbǎng zhōng,yǒu Hélán Huángjiā Qiàopái gōngsī,yě yǒu Měiguó de Wò'ěrmǎ.

赵　红：所以**“世界500强”**的排行榜中，有**荷兰皇家壳牌公司**，也有美国的**沃尔玛**。

Qí Yuǎn: Tīngshuō yī jiā zhōngguó de mínyíng qǐyè yě rùxuǎn le " wǔbǎi qiáng ".

齐　远：听说一家中国的**民营**企业也**入选**了“500强”。

Zhào Hóng: Zhōngguó dàxíng guóqǐ Zhōngshíhuà hái jìn le qián shí wèi ne.

赵　红：中国大型国企中石化还进了前十位呢。

Bǐ'ěr: Zhōngguó qǐyè qǔdé de zhèxiē chéngjiù yīnggāi hé Zhōngguó de rúshāng wénhuà yǒu guānxì ba?

比　尔：中国企业取得的这些**成就**应该和中国的**儒商**文化有关系吧？

Mǎ Lì: Rúshāng wénhuà?Zhè shì yī zhòng shénmeyàng de qǐyè wénhuà ne?

马　莉：儒商文化？这是一种什么样的企业文化呢？

Qí Yuǎn: Wǒ juéde rúshāng shì yǐ rújiā sīxiǎng wéi zhǐdǎo,fēicháng zhòngshì shāngyè dàodé de shāngrén.

齐 远：我觉得儒商是以**儒家思想**为指导，非常重视商业**道德**的**商人**。

Zhào Hóng: Tāmen shíxíng rénxìnghuà de guǎnlǐ, jùyǒu qiángliè de shèhuì zérèngǎn.

赵 红：他们**实行人性化**的管理，具有**强烈**的社会**责任感**。

Bǐ'ěr: Wǒ tīngshuō guò yìxiē guānyú Zhōngguó de jìnshāng hé huīshāng de gùshì, tāmen cháng shuō de yí jù huà jiào shénme láizhe……, xiǎng qǐlái le! "Jūnzǐ'àicái ,qǔzhīyǒudào ".

比 尔：我听说过一些关于中国的**晋商**和**徽商**的故事，他们常说的一句话叫什么来着……，想起来了！**"君子爱财，取之有道"**。

Qí Yuǎn: A,nǐ kuài chéng Zhōngguótōng le!

齐 远：啊，你快成**中国通**了！

Zhào Hóng: Xiànzài zhōngguó yǒu hěn duō qǐyèjiā zài xué guóxué,bǎ Zhōngguó de chuántǒng zhìhuì yùnyòng dào shāngwù guǎnlǐ hé yíngxiāo zhōng qù.

赵 红：现在中国有很多企业家在学**国学**，把中国的**传统智慧运用**到商务管理和营销中去。

Bǐ'ěr: Shì'a,wǒ yǐqián de shāngwù yíngxiāo kè lǎoshī shuōguò,《Sūnzǐ Bīngfǎ》shì yōuxiù de xiàndài qǐyè guǎnlǐzhě de bì bèi zhī shū.

比 尔：是啊，我以前的商务营销课老师说过，《孙子兵法》是**优秀**的现代企业管理者的**必备**之书。

Text 2

Corporate cultures are distinctly different

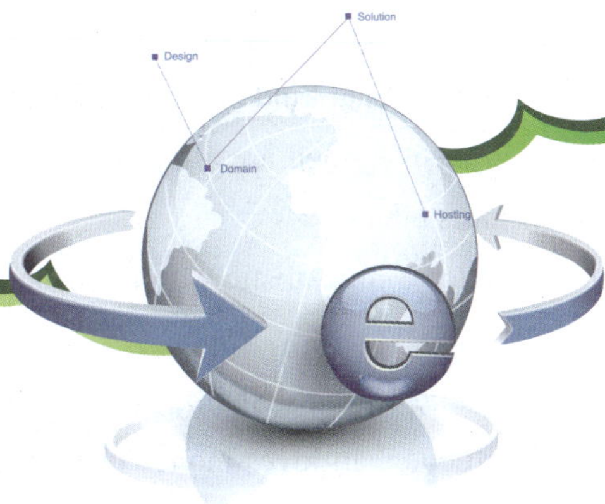

Bill, Zhao Hong, Maria and Qi Yuan are eating and chatting at a friend's party.

Bill:I have heard there are many Chinese college graduates who choose to work in foreign enterprises, why is that?

Maria: Because there are more and more foreign enterprises. (Maria smiles.)

Zhao Hong: It is generally recognized that employees of the foreign enterprises have higher salaries, excellent benefits, and plenty of career development opportunities. Besides, they may come into contact with a more sophisticated management system.

Maria: In different foreign enterprises, the corporate cultures are distinctly different.

Qi Yuan: That's right. One of my friends works in a Japanese company; he is very well paid, but the management is very strict and you have to obey your superiors absolutely.

Zhao Hong: Is it the same with Korean companies? One of my friends works in a Korean company; he often complains that they don't have enough opportunities for promotion and they always work overtime.

Qi Yuan: Hey Maria, do European companies have the same kind of corporate culture as American ones?

Maria: Not exactly the same. I think American companies are more concerned with their profits.

Zhao Hong: Aren't European companies concerned with profits as well?

Maria: Yes they are! But they believe that customers' needs and the company's profits are equally important.

Bill: The corporate culture of any country has its advantages.

Zhao Hong: Therefore among the Fortune Global 500 we have Royal Dutch Shell and Wal Mart from the US as well.

Qi Yuan: I have heard one of China's private enterprises has also been ranked among the Fortune Global 500.

Zhao Hong: And China's giant state enterprise Sinopec has even been ranked among the top ten.

Bill: The achievements of the Chinese enterprises may be connected with China's Confucian business heritage, right?

Maria: Confucian business heritage? What kind of corporate culture is that?

Qi Yuan: I think the Confucian businessmen are under the guidance of Confucian ideas, and they attach great importance to business ethics.

Zhao Hong: They put into practice a humanistic way of management, and they all have a strong sense of social responsibility.

Bill: I've heard some stories about China's Shanxi businessmen and Anhui businessmen, they often say…, oh I got it! "A virtuous man loves money as anybody may, but he gets his share in a righteous way."

Qi Yuan: Oh, you are almost an old China hand!

Zhao Hong: Now many Chinese entrepreneurs are studying the Chinese Learning, applying traditional Chinese wisdom in business management and marketing.

Bill: Right, my former teacher of Marketing said, *The Art of War* is a must read for high level managers of modern enterprises.

生词 New words

1	接触	jiēchù	to come into contact with
2	明显	míngxiǎn	distinctly
3	差别	chābié	difference
4	严格	yángé	rigid,strict
5	上司	shàngsi	boss, superior
6	绝对	juéduì	utterly
7	服从	fúcóng	to obey,subjection

8	抱怨	bàoyuàn	to complain
9	晋升	jìnshēng	to promote
10	老	lǎo	always
11	关心	guānxīn	to be concerned with
12	盈利	yínglì	profit
13	需求	xūqiú	needs
14	可取之处	kěqǔzhīchù	a saving grace
15	民营	mínyíng	to run by the local people
16	入选	rùxuǎn	to be selected; to be chosen
17	成就	chéngjiù	achievement
18	儒商	rúshāng	Confucian businessmen
19	儒家	rújiā	the Confucianists
20	思想	sīxiǎng	ideas
21	道德	dàodé	ethics
22	商人	shāngrén	businessman
23	实行	shíxíng	to put into practise
24	人性化的	rénxìnghuà	humanistic
25	强烈	qiángliè	strong, intense
26	责任感	zérèn gǎn	responsibility
27	晋商	jìnshāng	Shanxi businessmen
28	徽商	huīshāng	Anhui businessmen
29	君子爱财，取之有道	jūnzǐ àicái, qǔzhīyǒudào	a virtuous man loves money as anybody may, but he gets his share in a righteous way
30	中国通	zhōngguótōng	a foreigner who is familiar with the situation of China,old China hand
31	国学	guóxué	Chinese traditional culture, the Chinese Learning
32	传统	chuántǒng	tradition
33	智慧	zhìhuì	wisdom
34	运用	yùnyòng	to apply, to put to use
35	优秀	yōuxiù	excellent
36	必备	bìbèi	essential,necessary
37	之	zhī	the structural particle, same as “de(的)”

专有名词 Proper nouns

1. 日企
   Rìqǐ
   Japanese enterprises
   日本企业（全称）
   Rìběn qǐyè
2. 韩国
   Hánguó
   The Republic of Korea
3. 荷兰皇家壳牌（集团）
   Hélán Huángjiā Qiàopái（Jítuán）
   Royal Dutch /Shell Group of Companies
4. 沃尔玛
   Wò'ěrmǎ
   Wal-Mart Stores, Inc.
5. 中石化
   Zhōngshíhuà
   Sinopec Group
   中国石油化工集团（全称）
   Zhōngguó Shíyóu Huàgōng Jítuán
   China Petro-chemical Corporation
6. 《孙子兵法》
   《Sūnzǐ Bīngfǎ》
   The Art of War

注释 Notes

1. 他常常抱怨他们晋升的机会不多，还老加班。

He often complains that they don't have enough opportunities to get promoted and they always work overtime.

"老"，副词，经常，总是。例如：

"老", adverb, means "often", "always". For example:

（1）他上班老迟到。

He is always late for work.

（2）这个孩子老感冒。

This child often catches a cold.

（3）我的朋友老买法国货。

My friend always buys French products.

2. 我觉得美国公司更关心是否盈利。

I think American companies are more concerned with their profits.

"是否"，副词，是不是。例如：

"是否", adverb, means "whether or not". For example:

（1）明天是否下雨？

Will it rain tomorrow?

（2）他们是否来中国旅行，我还不确定。

I'm not sure whether they will travel here in China.

（3）我想知道你下周是否出席会议。

I'm wondering whether you will be present at the meeting next week.

3. 所以"世界500强"的排行榜中，有荷兰皇家壳牌公司，也有美国的沃尔玛。

Therefore among the Fortune Global 500 we have Royal Dutch Shell and Wal Mart from the US as well.

"世界500强"，是中国人对美国《财富》杂志每年评选的"全球最大五百家公司"排行榜的一种约定俗成的叫法。

1929年美国人亨利•卢斯在经济萧条的背景下创办了《财富》杂志，他认为商业文化是一个社会的核心，期望借助《财富》杂志为低迷的经济描绘出未来的希望。《财富》杂志被很多人关注，是因为它每年评出"全球最大五百家公司"，中国人习惯称他们为"世界五百强"。

《财富》杂志还评选"美国最大五百家公司"(也称为"财富五百强")、美国和全球最受赞赏的公司、美国青年富豪榜排行榜、全球商界最具权势25位企业家等一系列排名。同时，《财富》杂志还举办"《财富》全球论坛"，目前已经在中国上海、香港和北京举办过三届。

和同样推出公司排行榜的《福布斯》和《商业周刊》相比，《财富》的500强以销售收入为依据进行排名，比较重视企业规模。而《商业周刊》是把市值作为主要依据;《福布斯》则综合考虑年销售额、利润、总资产和市值。另外，《福布斯》的500强排名不包括美国公司。《商业周刊》的排名仅限于发达国家，而《财富》则将世界各国的企业都进行排名。

"世界500强" is how the Chinese customarily call the annual ranking list "Fortune Global 500" put together by *Fortune* magazine of the US.

In 1929 an American Henry Luce founded *Fortune* magazine in the backdrop of the economic recession. He regarded business culture as the core value of a society, wishing to depict a promising future for the still recessive economy. The *Fortune* magazine has been very much paid attention to, because it publishes an annual list of "Fortune Global 500".

Fortune magazine also lists "Fortune 500", "The Most Admired Companies" in US and the World, the Richest Americans under 40, the World's 25 Most Powerful People in Business. In the meanwhile, the *Fortune* magazine holds a "Fortune Global Forum", so far three times in the Chinese cities of Shanghai, Hong Kong and Beijing.

Comparing lists provided by *Forbes* and *BusinessWeek*, Fortune 500 are ranked according to sales revenues with importance attached to the size of companies. *BusinessWeek* takes the market value of a company as the major criterion; *Forbes* takes into consideration annual sales revenue, profit, total assets and market value. In addition, Forbes 500 does not include American companies. The ranking of *BusinessWeek* is confined to developed countries, while *Fortune* ranks enterprises of the whole world.

4. 他们以儒家思想为指导。

They are under the guidance of Confucian ideas.

"以"，介词，"以……为……"，介词短语，"把……作为，认为……"。例如：

"以", preposition; "以……为……", prepositional phrase, meaning "take…as, regard…". For example:

（1）在学习上，我一直以我的哥哥为榜样。

In studies I have always taken my elder brother as a role model.

（2）我们的公司以信誉至上为首要目标。

Our company regards High Credibility as the major objective.

（3）他以“失败是成功之母”为座右铭。

His motto is “Failure breeds success.”

5. “君子爱财，取之有道”。

“A virtuous man loves money as anybody may, but he gets his share in a righteous way”.

“君子爱财，取之有道，用之有度”。君子，指有才德、正直的人。有道，指合乎道义。君子喜欢正道得到的财物，不要不义之财。在中国传统文化中，人们常用这句话表示：人们在追求财富和赚钱的时候，应该合乎法律和道德的要求，不该为了钱财而做违反道义的事情。

“A virtuous man loves money as anybody may, but he gets his share in a righteous way and spends it in accordance with propriety.” “君子” refers to a man of virtue or a righteous man. “有道” means complying with righteousness. A man of virtue loves money acquired in a righteous way and rejects money of unrighteousness. In traditional Chinese culture, people use this expression to say that one's pursuit of fortune should not run against law or morality and that one should not do unrighteous things for the sake of money.

6. 啊，你快成中国通了！

Oh, you are almost an old China hand!

中国通，现在我们常常用来指非常熟悉中国情况的外国人，比如说对中国的自然地理、各地的风俗习惯都很了解。也指研究中国问题的专家。例如：

中国通, with which we usually refer to a foreigner who is very familiar with China such as geography and local customs. It may also refer to an expert of Chinese issues. For example:

他在中国生活了七八年，可以说是个中国通了。

He has been living in China for seven or eight years; he may very well be called a China hand.

7. 中国有很多企业家在学国学。

Many Chinese entrepreneurs are studying the Chinese Learning.

“国学”，可以音译为“gúoxué”。意译，有人翻译为Sinology(意思是指中国学，汉学)。国学原来指国家学府，如太学、国子监。国学用来指学问一说，产生于西方学术文化思想传入东方，中国文化转型的历史时期。20世纪初梁启超、章太炎等人提出国学的概念时，国学指的是“相对于西方学术的本国传统学术”，主要内容是小学，还有经学，包括经史子集。

小学，包括训诂、文字、音韵，指研究中国古代汉语的词义、文字、语音等。经史子集，“经”指古代社会中的政教、纲常伦理、道德规范的教条，主要是儒家的著作。“史”是指历史方面著作，“子”是指春秋战国以来各种学说的著作。“集”是指古代诗文词赋的著作。

按照国学大师章太炎《国学讲演录》的划分，分为小学、经学、史学、诸子和文学。按照思想来分，分为先秦诸子、儒道释三家等，儒家思想贯穿并主导中国思想史，其他的是从属地位。但是到了后来，特别是20世纪八九十年代以后，国学这个词的意思就不是很严格，只要是传统文化内容似乎都可以叫做国学。这也是在一般人心目中“国学”的含义。因此，广义上说，历史、思想、哲学、地理、政治、经济乃至书画、音乐、术数、医学、星相、建筑等都是国学所涉及的范畴。

“国学” , may be transliterated as “guoxue”. Semantically, some translate it as Sinology. Guoxue originally refers to the state academy, such as Taixue, Guozijian. Guoxue was borrowed to refer to a school of learning when the western culture was imported to China causing a transition of the Chinese culture. At the beginning of the 20th century, Liang Qichao and Zhang Taiyan proposed the concept of Chinese Learning, which means the Chinese traditional learning as the counterpart of Western academics, including scriptures, histories, masters and collections with primary studies and scriptures studies as the main content.

Primary studies includes semantics, characters and pronunciation, the study of meaning, characters and pronunciation of ancient Chinese language. “Scriptures” refers to the teachings of politics and ethics in the ancient society, mainly the works of Confucianism. “Histories” refers to writings of history. “Masters” refers to the works of different schools of thought since the periods of the Spring and Autumn, and the Warring States. “Collections” refers to the works of ancient poetry and essays.

According to Zhang Taiyan’s *Lectures on the Chinese Learning*, the Chinese Learning may be divided into primary studies, scriptures, histories, masters and literature. According to the criteria of ideas, the Chinese Learning may be divided into Confucianism, Buddhism and Taosim with Confucianism as the mainstream. Later, especially since 1980s or 1990s, the meaning of Chinese Learning has not been so strictly defined, anything of the traditional Chinese culture can be called Chinese Learning, which is a common understanding among the general public. Therefore, in a broader sense, the Chinese Learning involves history, thought, geography, politics, economics, calligraphy and painting, music, numerology, medicine, astrology and architecture.

8.《孙子兵法》是优秀的现代企业管理者的必备之书。

***The Art of War* is a must read for high level managers of modern enterprises.**

《孙子兵法》是中国最早的一部兵书，主要讲述军事战略和战术。

《孙子兵法》既是中国古代最伟大的军事理论著作，也是中国优秀文化传统的重要组成部分，是中国在世界上影响最大、最为广泛的著作之一。后来，书中的谋略、哲学思想也被运用在企业经营管理中。

The Art of War is one of the earliest books on military strategies. It is not only the greatest book of military theories in ancient China, but also one of the most influential Chinese books in the world as part of the Chinese cultural heritage. Later the strategic and philosophic ideas of the book are also used in the management of enterprises.

练习 Exercises

一、跟读生词并且纠音。
Read the new words after the teacher and correct your pronunciation.

二、跟读课文并且纠音。
Read the text after the teacher and correct your pronunciation.

三、学生分组，分角色朗读课文一、二。
Divide the students into groups and read the texts 1 & 2 in different roles.

四、学生分组，不看书分角色表演课文一、二。
Divide the students into groups and role play texts 1 & 2 without referring to the book.

五、根据课文，回答下面问题。
Answer the following questions according to the text.

课文一：

1. 什么事情让马莉头疼？
2. 为什么很多外企喜欢录用本土人才？
3. 文中谈到了哪几个公司的“本土化”？他们是怎么实施“本土化”的？

课文二：

1. 为什么很多毕业生喜欢去外企工作？
2. 文中谈到在日企、韩企的工作如何？
3. 欧洲公司和美国公司的管理一样吗？
4. 在管理文化上，欧洲公司和美国公司有什么差异？
5. 什么是儒商文化？
6. 你怎么理解“君子爱财，取之有道”？
7. 为什么有些中国企业家在研究国学？

六、角色扮演。
Role play.

请使用课文中学习过的汉语词语和句子。

1. 3-4人一组，分别扮演一家在中国的外资公司的CEO、人力资源经理、市场经理、销售经理，讨论该公司将如何实行“本土化”。

2. 3-4人一组，分别扮演日本公司、美国公司、德国公司、法国公司的职员或经理，谈论本公司的员工福利与培训计划、办公室文化、公司的管理，甚至上司的工作特点等相关的企业文化。

七、把下面的词语组成句子。
Make a sentence with the following groups of words.

课文一：

1. 外企　很多　人才　喜欢　录用　本土
2. 做得　很　我　成功　觉得　公司　Coco Cola
3. 可口可乐　在中国　名字　家喻户晓　这个
4. 顾客　为　服务　他们　方便　了　更　的　提供
5. 适合　推出　的　肯德基　品种　中国人　不断　口味　新

课文二：

1. 大学 选择 很多 去 毕业生 工作 外企
2. 文化 明显 企业 也 的 差别 有
3. 常常 他 晋升 不多 的 机会 抱怨
4. 同样 客户 和 需求 重要 的 盈利 公司 的
5. 儒商 责任感 具有 的 社会 强烈

八、根据课文内容，完成下面的句子。

Complete the following sentences according to the text.

课文一：

1. 你可以把这些工作外包给____________________。
2. 很多外企喜欢录用本土人才，还因为____________________。
3. 摩托罗拉____________________________高达80%。

课文二：

4. 一般人认为，外企的中国员工________，____________________，__________，还可以____________________。
5. 不同的外企，__________________也有着明显的差别。
6. 我觉得美国公司更关心__________________。
7. 一般来说，欧洲公司觉得____________和____________同样重要。
8. 我觉得儒商是以____________为指导，非常重视__________的商人。
9. 很多企业家在学国学，把____________运用到商务____________中去。
10. 《孙子兵法》是优秀的_______________的必备之书。

九、用括号里的词语完成句子。

Complete the sentence with the words in the brackets.

1. 他喜欢旅行，去过很多国家和地区，__________________。（比如说）
2. 注册公司需要准备一些相关文件，__________________。（比如说）
3. 去年两国的双边贸易额____________________。（高达）

4. 我们的产品品种齐全，________________。（多达）
5. 最近我的电脑出了点问题，________________。（老）
6. 他常常抱怨________________。（老）
7. ________________，我还不知道。（是否）
8. 这次会议讨论了________________。（是否）
9. 比尔·盖茨________________。（家喻户晓）
10. ________________是很必要的。（风土人情）
11. 找工作时，________________。（重视）
12. ________________，所以被老板辞退了。（服从）

十、选词填空。
Choose the words given below to fill in the blanks.

头疼　本土化　运用　明显　外包　实行　需求
品种　责任感　抱怨　入选　盈利　必备　严格

1. 很多跨国企业都采用了（　　）战略。
2. 大厅里摆着（　　）繁多的盆花。
3. 一般的公司（　　）五天工作制。
4. 在开发新产品前，我们先了解了一下市场（　　）。
5. 目前令政府（　　）的是失业率不断上升。
6. 他一向（　　）要求自己的子女。
7. 他对工作尽心尽力，有着强烈的（　　）。
8. 上海曾（　　）全球十大最具发展潜力城市。
9. 发达国家和发展中国家存在（　　）的差距。
10. 这家企业本季度实现（　　）170万元。
11. 如何把知识（　　）到实践中是一门学问。
12. 员工总是（　　）工作环境不够舒适。
13. 很多大品牌电脑公司把一部分业务（　　）给小公司。
14. 对于一个经理人来说，基本的财务和法律知识是（　　）的。

十一、商务案例分析。
Business case analysis.

案例（一）

材料一

1988年，**雀巢**（quècháo, Nestle）公司正式进军中国市场。1990年，第一家合资工厂开始运营，随后又建立了多家工厂。目前雀巢在中国销售的产品中99%是在本地制造的。现在雀巢公司在中国的销售额已经超过100亿人民币。

材料二

2001年，雀巢在上海成立**研发**（yánfā, research and development）中心。主要研究并开发中国消费者喜爱的、适合中国人口味和消费能力的**营养**（yíngyǎng, nutritious）食品。

材料三

雀巢在中国消费者中如此家喻户晓，**得益于**（déyìyú, to profit from）早期广告中的"雀巢，味道好极了"，深入人心。雀巢用广告等多种方法，来宣传喝咖啡是一种时尚、潮流，成功地**吸引**（xīyǐn, to attract）了一群年轻人。

材料四

雀巢最初进入中国时，产品采用的是礼品装，因为中国人会在节日和看望亲友时送礼，雀巢咖啡被当作"外国的高级礼品"走进了中国人的家庭，逐渐咖啡市场**培育**（péiyù, to breed）起来，现在的1+2方便装成为市场主要产品。

1.请先阅读上面的4份材料，然后以雀巢公司为例，小组讨论并说明雀巢公司在中国怎样进行"本土化"。

2.结合雀巢公司的经营活动，从生产本土化、人才本土化、营销本土化、产品本土化、管理本土化、运作本土化等方面来概括，完成一份雀巢公司"本土化"情况的总结。2-3人一组，分析讨论后，每组各做一份口头和书面的总结。

案例（二）

材料一

一位美国公司的电脑工程师说，"办公室是开放式的，每个人都很忙，不论职位高低，**一律**（yílǜ, without exception）直呼对方的英文名字，大家工作都很**拼命**（pīnmìng, going all out），通宵加班是常事。入职后，有各种各样的培训项目可以参加。每个人看起来都有工作热情和十足的自信。"

材料二

在德国公司工作的路易莎认为，德国企业文化简单大方，员工自由度高，上班不用**打卡**（dǎkǎ, punch in/out），待遇很好，而且压力小，几乎不加班，懂得**享受**（xiǎngshòu, to enjoy）生活，**工作狂**（gōngzuòkuáng, workaholic）比较少见。

材料三

在日企工作的Tom Chen 介绍说，日企**讲究**（jiǎngjiū, be particular about）合作、团结，下级服从上级，几乎个个都是工作狂。但是福利待遇相当好，企业的氛围好像家一样温暖，**业余**（yèyú, after-hours）活动多种多样。

材料四

在韩资企业的李经理说：“公司管理严格，每周工作六天，培训计划也很多，只是中国人在公司的地位低于韩国人，所以晋升的机会不多，待遇也比不上韩国人。”

1.阅读上面材料完成下面表格。

	管理严格	经常加班	等级分明	压力大	待遇高	员工平等	培训多
日企							
韩企							
美资公司							
德国公司							

2.结合上述表格内容，2～4人一组完成情景对话，对不同的企业管理文化进行评价，每个人都要提出自己的看法。

十二、复述课文一和课文二。
Retell the texts 1 & 2.

十三、完成任务。
Complete the following tasks.

1.请向你的同学们举例说明你的国家的某个企业的管理文化。

2.小组任务：

说明：3～4人一组，选定一家或两家在中国的跨国公司，收集相关资料，总结分析它们在中国的“本土化”经营情况，提出自己的看法。最后各组到课堂上来向同学和老师做报告。小组报告可以在下面选择一种方式。

小组报告的方式：

（1）小组选出一位代表来作陈述。

（2）小组成员一起编排一个对话来表演。

Unit 3

第三单元

Zhāobiāo

招标

Tender

课文一

Wo zhèngzài kàn zhège zhāobiāo gōnggào ne

我正在看这个招标公告呢

Qí Yuǎn zhèngzài jiāli kàn bàozhǐ, tā bèi shìzhèngfǔ bàngōng shèbèi cǎigòu de zhāobiāo gōnggào xīyǐn zhù le. Bǐ'ěr lái zhǎo tā, qiāo le bàntiān mén, tā cái tīngjiàn.

齐远正在家里看报纸，他被市政府办公设备采购的招标公告吸引住了。比尔来找他，敲了半天门，他才听见。

Bǐ'ěr: Zěnme zhème cháng shíjiān cái kāimén, wǒ hái yǐwéi nǐ búzài jiā ne.

比　尔：怎么这么长时间才开门，我还以为你不在家呢！

Qí Yuǎn: Bàoqiàn! Wǒ zhèngzài kàn zhège zhāobiāo gōnggào ne, méi tīngjiàn nǐ qiāomén.

齐　远：抱歉！我正在看这个**招标公告**呢，没听见你敲门。

Bǐ'ěr: Shénme zhāobiāo gōnggào ràng nǐ zhème rùmí?

比　尔：什么招标公告让你这么**入迷**？

Qí Yuǎn: Shìzhèngfǔ yào cǎigòu yì pī bàngōng shèbèi. Hē shénme?

齐　远：市政府要采购一批办公设备。喝什么？

Bǐ'ěr: Suíbiàn! Zhè kěshì yì bǐ dà shēngyi. Nǐmen gōngsī kěndìng huì tóubiāo ba?

比　尔：随便！这可是一笔大生意。你们公司肯定会投标吧？

Qí Yuǎn: Wǒ xiǎng míngtiān xiàng gōngsī tí chū tóubiāo de jiànyì,bùguò wǒ xiànzài yǒu diǎn dānxīn……（Qí Yuǎn dì gěi Bǐ'ěr yì bēi chá）chángcháng péngyou sòng de xīn chá.

齐　远：我想明天向公司提出**投标**的建议，不过我现在有点担心……（齐远递给比尔一杯茶）尝尝朋友送的新茶！

Bǐ'ěr: Hǎo!（Bǐ'ěr jiē guò chá） Nǐ dānxīn shénme?

比　尔：好！（比尔接过茶）你担心什么？

Qí Yuǎn: Nǐ zhīdào ma, xiāoshòu bàngōng shèbèi de gōngsī tèbié duō. Xiàng zhèyàng de zhāobiāo xiàngmù, dìjiāo shūmiàn tóubiāo yìxiàng de qǐmǎ jiù yǒu shàng bǎi jiā. Zīgé yùshěn wán le zuìduō shèng xià èrshí lái jiā. Yìbān jiù kāi chū wǔ ge biāo, jìngbiāo shí, hái yào wǔ xuǎn yī.

齐　远：你知道吗，销售办公设备的公司特别多。像这样的招标项目，**递交书面**投标**意向**的**起码**就有上百家。**资格预审**完了最多剩下20来家。一般就开出5个标，竞标时，还要五选一。

Bǐ'ěr: Zhēn shì bǎilǐ tiāo yī.

比　尔：真是**百里挑一**。

Qí Yuǎn: Shì ya, jìngzhēng zhème jīliè, wǒ néng bù dānxīn ma?

齐　远：是呀，竞争这么激烈，我能不担心吗？

Bǐ'ěr: Zhè dàoshì,bùguò, nǐmen bùfáng shì yíxià. Qítā de gōngsī yě bù yídìng yǒu shízú de bǎwò.

比　尔：这倒是，不过，你们**不妨**试一下。其他的公司也不一定有**十足**的把握。

Qí Yuǎn: Nǐ shuō de yǒu dàolǐ, wǒmen shì yīnggāi shì yíxià.

齐　远：你说得有道理，我们是应该试一下。

Bǐ'ěr: Tóubiāo de zhǔnbèi gōngzuò máfan ma?
比　尔：投标的准备工作麻烦吗？

Qí Yuǎn: Bú suàn tài máfan,jiùshì yào zhǔnbèi yìxiē tóubiāo de wénjiàn. Nǐ kàn, zhège gōnggào shàng shuō: tóubiāorén yào tígōng yíngyè zhízhào fùběn、shuìwù dēngjìzhèng fùběn、fǎdìng dàibiǎorén zhèngmíngshū huò shòuquán wěituōshū……（Tāmen liǎng rén zhèngzài dú bàozhǐ shàng de zhāobiāo gōnggào.）
齐　远：不算太麻烦，就是要准备一些投标的文件。你看，这个公告上说：**投标人**要提供**营业执照副本**、**税务登记证副本**、**法定**代表人证明书或**授权**委托书……（他们两人正在读报纸上的招标公告。）

Bǐ'ěr: Zhèr háiyǒu, jìn jǐ nián de yèjì bàogào、yínháng zīxìn zhèngmíng děng wénjiàn、zhuānyè rényuán děng de xìnxī……
比　尔：这儿还有，近几年的**业绩**报告、银行资信证明等文件、专业技术人员等的信息……

Qí Yuǎn: Zhǐyǒu tōngguò Zhāobiāo Wěiyuánhuì de yùshěn, wǒmen cái néng huòdé cānyǔ tóubiāo de zīgé.
齐　远：只有通过**招标委员会**的预审，我们才能获得**参与**投标的资格。

Bǐ'ěr: Hái yào mǎi biāoshū ba?
比　尔：还要买**标书**吧？

Qí Yuǎn: Dāngrán,guì zhe ne.
齐　远：当然，贵着呢。

Bǐ'ěr: Shénme shíhou kāibiāo?
比　尔：什么时候**开标**？

Qí Yuǎn: Chàbuduō háiyǒu yí ge yuè.
齐　远：差不多还有一个月。

Bǐ'ěr: Zhǐyào ná dìng zhǔyi, jiù kěyǐ zhuóshǒu zhǔnbèi le.
比　尔：只要拿定主意，就可以**着手**准备了。

Qí Yuǎn: Wǒ míngtiān jiù xiàng lǎobǎn tí chū jiànyì.
齐　远：我明天就向老板提出建议。

Bǐ'ěr: Jiāyóu!
比　尔：加油！

Text 1

I was reading the tender notice

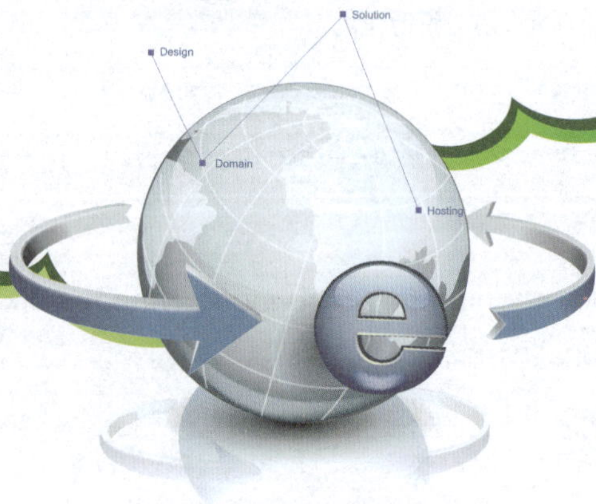

Qi Yuan is reading newspapers at home. He is absorbed in the tender notice for office equipment by the municipal government. Bill knocks at the door for quite a while before Qi hears.

Bill: What took you so long? I thought you were not home!

Qi Yuan: Sorry! I was reading this tender notice. I didn't hear your knocking.

Bill: What tender notice makes you so fascinated?

Qi Yuan: The municipal government is planning to purchase office equipment. Any drinks?

Bill: Whatever! This is a big business opportunity. Your company will surely bid for it, right?

Qi Yuan: I will propose a bid tomorrow, but I'm a bit worried…(*Qi Yuan gives Bill a cup of tea.*) Have a taste of this new tea my friend sent me!

Bill: Good! (*Bill takes the cup of tea.*) What do you worry about?

Qi Yuan: You know, there are too many companies selling office equipment. For a tender like this, the number of companies submitting letters of bidding intent will be 100. Only about 20 will be left after the preliminary qualification process and generally there are only five bidders when the bids are opened. At the bidding you have to be the winner out of the five.

Bill: It's really one out of a hundred.

Qi Yuan: Yes, the competition is so fierce. How can't I worry?

Bill: That's understandable, but you might as well have a try. Other companies may not be very confident either.

Qi Yuan: You are right. We should have a try.

Bill: Is it complicated to prepare for the bidding?

Qi Yuan: It's not very complicated; some bidding documents need to be prepared. Look, the notice here says: a bidder shall provide a copy of business license, a copy of tax registration certificate, certificate of legal representative or letter of authorization…(*They are reading the tender notice in the newspaper.*)

Bill: In addition to that, other documents include performance reports of recent years, bank reference letters, and information of professional and technical personnel, …

Qi Yuan: Only when we pass the preliminary qualification process of the tender committee can we acquire the qualification for bidding.

Bill: And you have to buy the bidding papers, right?

Qi Yuan: Of course, and it's very expensive.

Bill: When will the bids be opened?

Qi Yuan: About a month from now.

Bill: If you're determined to do it, you may start to make preparations now.

Qi Yuan: I will put forward my proposal to the boss tomorrow.

Bill: Go ahead, man!

生词 New words

1	招标	zhāobiāo	to invite tenders
2	公告	gōnggào	notice
3	入迷	rùmí	be fascinated
4	投标	tóubiāo	to enter a bid
5	递交	dìjiāo	to hand over
6	书面	shūmiàn	in written form
7	意向	yìxiàng	intention
8	起码	qǐmǎ	at least
9	资格	zīgé	qualification
10	预审	yùshěn	the preliminary qualification process
11	百里挑一	bǎlǐtiāoyī	one out of a hundred
12	不妨	bùfáng	might as well
13	十足	shízú	pure,downright

14	投标人	tóubiāorén	a bidder; a tenderer
15	营业	yíngyè	to do business
16	执照	zhízhào	licence
17	副本	fùběn	a copy
18	税务	shuìwù	tax
19	登记证	dēngjìzhèng	registration
20	法定	fǎdìng	legal
21	授权	shòuquán	to empower,to authorize
22	业绩	yèjì	performance
23	参与	cānyǔ	to participate in
24	标书	biāoshū	bidding papers
25	开标	kāibiāo	to open sealed tenders
26	着手	zhuóshǒu	to set about

专有名词 Proper nouns

市政府
Shìzhèngfǔ
Municipal government

招标委员会
Zhāobiāo Wěiyuánhuì
Tender Board

注释 Notes

1．递交书面投标意向的起码就有上百家。

The number of companies submitting letters of bidding intent will be 100.

"上"，这里是动词，表示达到一定数量或者程度。可以放在百、千、万等数字的前面。例如：上千家公司、上万名留学生。

"上", here a verb, meaning "reaching a certain amount or degree", usually put before numbers such as "hundred", "thousand", or "ten thousand" etc. For example: as many as a thousand companies, as many as ten thousand overseas students.

2．资格预审完了最多剩下20来家。

Only about 20 will be left after the preliminary qualification process.

"来"是助词，用在十、百、千、万等数词的后面，表示概数。例如：三百来所学校、五千来人、两万来块钱、七十来岁。

"来", an auxiliary, used after such numbers as "ten", "hundred", "thousand" or "ten thousand", indicating an approximate amount. For example: about three hundred schools, about five thousand people, about twenty thousand Yuan, about seventy of age.

3．真是百里挑一。

It's really one out of a hundred.

"百里挑一"是说从100个里边挑出1个，比喻十分出众。也可以用"千里挑一"、"万里挑一"来表示更加强调。例如：

"百里挑一", literally means to choose one from a hundred, indicating "very outstanding". "千里挑一" or "万里挑一" may also be used to emphasize. For example:

她可是一个万里挑一的好姑娘。

She is a good girl, one out of ten thousand.

4．这倒是，不过，你们不妨试一下。

That's understandable, but you might as well have a try.

"这倒是，不过……" 这个句式常在口语里出现，表示先同意前边说的，然后再表达转折的意思。"不过"比"但是"的语气轻一些。例如：

"这倒是，不过……", the pattern usually appears in oral Chinese, indicating a concessive agreement first followed by a turn in meaning. Compared with "但是", "不过" sounds a bit softer. For example:

（1）学生也不能每天只知道学习呀。

Even students can not just study everyday.

（2）这倒是，不过，对学生来说，学习是主要的任务。

That's right, but study is really the main task for students.

5．你们不妨试一下。

You might as well have a try.

"不妨"是副词，可以用来建议，表示可以这样做，没什么妨碍。例如：

"不妨", adverb,used to propose something, indicating "that may be done without any obstacles." For example:

（1）你有什么意见，不妨提出来。

Whatever opinions you have, just voice them.

（2）现在也没什么好办法，不妨听听他的意见。

We don't have any good measures now and we might as well listen to what he has to say.

（3）孩子有什么想法，不妨让他说出来。

Whatever ideas the boy may have, you might as well allow him to speak up.

6．当然，贵着呢。

Of course, and it's very expensive.

"……着呢"用在口语中，表示强调；也可以表示动作、情况正在进行，这时动词前可以加上"正"。例如：

"……着呢", used in oral Chinese, indicating an emphasis; it may also be used to mean that an action or situation is going on, in which case "正" may be put before the verb. For example:

（1）我家离学校远着呢。

My home is quite far from the school.

（2）妈妈做的饭香着呢。

My Mom cooks delicious food.

（3）他正高兴着呢。

He is very happy now.

7. 只要拿定主意，就可以着手准备了。

If you're determined to do it, you may start to make preparations now.

“拿主意”指决定处理事情的办法。“拿”的后面可以加“定”，表示已经决定了，不改了。例如：

“拿主意” means to make a decision about how to handle an issue. “拿” may be followed by “定”, indicating the decision has been made and won't be changed. For example:

（1）咱们参加不参加竞标，还得您拿主意。

Whether we should participate in the bidding is up to you.

（2）她拿定主意，明年春天去留学。

She has decided to study overseas next spring.

（3）你怎么还拿不定主意呀？

Why haven't you made up your mind?

课文二

Gōngxǐ nǐmen zhòngbiāo le

恭喜你们中标了

Jīngguò jīliè de jìngbiāo,Qí Yuǎn de gōngsī zhòngbiāo le. Xīnxǐ zhī yú, Qí Yuǎn qǐng Bǐ'ěr chīfàn.

经过激烈的竞标，齐远的公司中标了。欣喜之余，齐远请比尔吃饭。

Bǐ'ěr: Wǒ shuō shénme láizhe, dàdǎn chángshì, zhè bù jiù chénggōng le.
比　尔：我说什么来着，**大胆尝试**，这不就成功了。

Qí Yuǎn: Duōkuī nǐ gǔlì wǒ. Lái! Gān yì bēi!
齐　远：多亏你鼓励我。来！干一杯！

Bǐ'ěr: Kànlái nǐmen gōngsī háishì hěn yǒu shílì de. Qiān hétong le ma?
比　尔：看来你们公司还是很有实力的。签合同了吗？

Qí Yuǎn: Qiān dàoshì qiān le, jiùshì yǒuxiē tiáokuǎn bǐjiào kēkè.
齐　远：签倒是签了，就是有些条款比较**苛刻**。

Bǐ'ěr: Kèhù gòumǎi bàngōng shèbèi shí, búwàihu jiùshì kànzhòng chǎnpǐn de zhìliàng hé shòuhòu fúwù.
比　尔：客户购买办公设备时，不外乎就是**看重**产品的质量和售后服务。

Qí Yuǎn: Wǒmen xiāoshòu de bàngōng shèbèi shì dà pǐnpái, zhìliàng kěndìng méi wèntí, jiùshì shòuhòu fúwù fāngmiàn……
齐　远：我们销售的办公设备是大品牌，质量肯定没问题，就是售后服务方面……

Bǐ'ěr: Nǐmen de wéixiū lìliàng búshì méi wèntí ma?
比　尔：你们的**维修**力量不是没问题吗？

Qí Yuǎn: Jìshù zhīchí méi wèntí, kěshì hétong tiáokuǎn guīdìng, fùyìnjī、dǎyìnjī děng shèbèi de bǎoxiūqī tài cháng le. Wǒmen néng bǎozhèng shàngménfúwù,suíjiàosuídào, kěshì wéixiū chéngběn guò gāo.
齐　远：技术支持没问题，可是合同条款规定，**复印机**、**打印机**等设备的**保修**期太长了。我们能保证**上门服务**，随叫随到，可是维修成本过高。

Bǐ'ěr: Nǐmen dìng de chǎnpǐn jiàgé zěnmeyàng?
比　尔：你们定的产品价格怎么样？

Qí Yuǎn: Nǐ shì zhīdào de, tóubiāo shí bù néng tǎojiàhuánjià, wèile ràng gōngsī de bàojià zuì yǒu jìngzhēnglì, wǒmen bǎ jiàgé yāde hěn dī, lìrùn shǎo de kělián.
齐　远：你是知道的，投标时不能**讨价还价**，为了让公司的报价最有竞争力，我们把价格**压**得很低，利润少得可怜。

Bǐ'ěr: Wèile jìngbiāo, zhè yě méi bànfǎ.
比　尔：为了竞标，这也没办法。

Qí Yuǎn: Bùguò, zuò bàngōng shèbèi de shēngyi dàoshì yǒu ge tèdiǎn, jiùshì kěyǐ shùnbiàn mài xiē bàngōng hàocái, zhè dàoshì ge chángxiàn shēngyi.
齐　远：不过，做办公设备的生意倒是有个特点，就是可以顺便卖些办公**耗材**，这倒是个**长线**生意。

Bǐ'ěr: Duì, yóu nǐmen gōngsī fùzé tígōng hàocái de huà, jiù kěyǐ duō zhuàn yìxiē.
比　尔：对，由你们公司负责提供耗材的话，就可以多**赚**一些。

Qí Yuǎn: Shì ya, suīrán zuò hàocái lìrùn bù gāo,dàn duōshǎo kěyǐ míbǔ yíxià wéixiū chéngběn guò gāo de sǔnshī.
齐　远：是呀，虽然做耗材利润不高，但多少可以**弥补**一下维修成本过高的损失。

Bǐ'ěr: Kànlái háishì nǐ yǒu jīngjì tóunǎo.
比　尔：看来还是你有经济**头脑**。

Qí Yuǎn: Bié guāng gù shuōhuà, zánmen hē jiǔ ba.
齐　远：别光顾说话，咱们喝酒吧。

Bǐ'ěr: Hǎo, gōngxǐ nǐmen zhòngbiāo, gānbēi!
比　尔：好，恭喜你们中标，干杯！

Qí Yuǎn: Xièxie, gānbēi!
齐　远：谢谢，干杯！

Text 2

Congratulations on your successful bidding

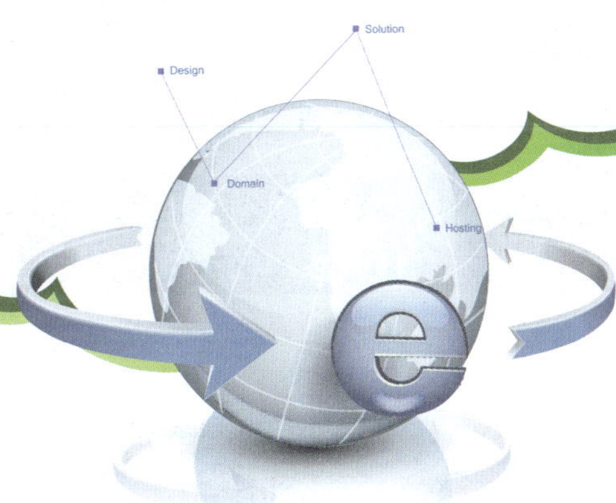

After a fierce bidding process, Qi Yuan's company wins the bid. In the spirit of happiness, Qi Yuan invites Bill to dinner.

Bill: Remember what I told you? Just be bold and have a try, and now you're the winner.

Qi Yuan: Thanks to your encouragement. Come on! Cheers!

Bill: It seems your company is quite competitive. Have you signed the contract?

Qi Yuan: Yes, we have. But some terms are a bit too harsh.

Bill: When a customer buys office equipment, his major concern is the quality of product and after sale service.

Qi Yuan: We sell big brands office equipment; the quality is unquestionable. But in the aspect of after-sales service……

Bill: Your maintenance abilities are quite good, aren't they?

Qi Yuan: Technical support is no problem, but the contract stipulates that the guarantee period for photocopier and printer etc. is rather long. And we have to guarantee a door-to-door service at any time, but the maintenance cost is too steep.

Bill: What about the prices you set for your products?

Qi Yuan: You know, you can't bargain in the bidding process. For competitive prices, we had to lower them to a level of minimal profit.

Bill: In order to win the bid, you cannot do otherwise.

Qi Yuan: But there is an aspect about the business of office equipment: you can sell consumables alongside, and that's a long-term business.

Bill: Right, if your company can supply the consumables, you can make more money.

Qi Yuan: Yes, though it's not quite profitable to sell consumables, it can make up some of the losses due to the high costs of maintenance.

Bill: It seems you do have the brain for business.

Qi Yuan: Let's not just talk; let's drink.

Bill: OK, congratulations on your successful bidding. Cheers!

Qi Yuan: Thank you. Cheers!

生词 New words

1	中标	zhòngbiāo	to win a bid
2	大胆	dàdǎn	bold
3	尝试	chángshì	to try
4	苛刻	kēkè	harsh
5	看重	kànzhòng	to regard as important
6	维修	wéixiū	to keep in repair
7	复印机	fùyìnjī	photocopier
8	打印机	dǎyìnjī	printer
9	保修	bǎoxiū	guarantee to keep sth.
10	上门服务	shàngménfúwù	door-to-door service
11	讨价还价	tǎojiàhuánjià	to bargain
12	压	yā	to press
13	耗材	hàocái	consumables
14	长线	chángxiàn	long term
15	赚	zhuàn	to earn (money)
16	弥补	míbǔ	to make up,to remedy
17	头脑	tóunǎo	brains

注释 Notes

1. 我说什么来着，大胆尝试，这不就成功了。

Remember what I told you? Just be bold and have a try, and now you're the winner.

"来着"是助词，用在口语中，表示曾经发生过什么事。例如：

"来着", is an auxiliary, used in oral Chinese, indicating something has already taken place. For example:

（1）他刚才说什么来着？

What did he say just now?

（2）他去年还去欧洲旅游来着。

He travelled to Europe just last year.

（3）你忘了马莉告诉咱们面试要注意什么来着。

Do you still remember what Mary told us about the dos and don'ts of an interview?

2. 多亏你鼓励我。

Thanks to your encouragement.

"多亏"是动词，表示由于别人的帮助或是某种有利因素，避免了不幸或是得到了好处。例如：

"多亏", verb, indicating something unlucky has been avoided or a benefit has been gained because of the help from others or some advantage. For example:

（1）多亏你叫醒我，否则我就迟到了。

Thanks to your waking me up, or I'd have been late.

（2）这件事多亏了大家的帮助。

Thanks to everybody's help, or I couldn't have made it.

（3）我能顺利通过面试，多亏了你们辅导我。

Thanks to your coaching, I have passed the interview successfully.

3. 客户购买办公设备时，不外乎就是看重产品的质量和售后服务。

When a customer buys office equipment, what he's most concerned about are nothing but the quality of product and after sale service.

"不外"，动词，也可以说"不外乎"，表示只包括这些，没有别的了。例如：

"不外", verb, also "不外乎", indicating only these are included, nothing else. For example:

（1）找工作不外乎就是看重待遇、工作环境、发展空间等。

In seeking a job, what we value are nothing but salary, working environment and development opportunities.

（2）我们聊的不外乎工作上的事儿。

What we talked aboutwere nothing but things concerned with our work.

（3）他爱吃的不外面条、饺子。

What he likes to eat art nothing but noodles and jiaozi.

4. 我们把价格压得很低，利润少得可怜。

We had to lower our prices to a level of minimal profit.

“可怜”这里是形容词，形容数量少或者质量差，不值得一提。作补语，前边一般带“得”。例如：

“可怜” here an adjective, describing a small amount or poor quality not worth mentioning. As a complement, it is usually preceded by “得”. For example:

（1）他会的生词少得可怜。

His vocabulary is pitiably small.

（2）那个地方的人穷得可怜。

The people there are pitiably poor.

（3）他们公司新员工的工资低得可怜。

The new employees of their company have a pitiably small salary.

5. 由你们公司负责提供耗材的话，就可以多赚一些。

If your company may supply the consumables, you can make more money.

“由”，这里是介词，引出动作的施行者，表示归谁去做。基本形式是：由+施动者+动词。例如：

“由”, a preposition, introducing the agent of the verb, indicating who conducts the act. The basic pattern is: “由”+agent+verb. For example:

（1）我们的班长由齐远担任。

The position of monitor was held by Qi Yuan.

（2）这次活动是由马莉组织的。

The activity was organized by Maria.

（3）喜津服装公司的刘总经理由小张陪同。

Mr. Liu, general manager of Xijin Garment, was accompanied by Xiaozhang.

6. 虽然做耗材利润不高，但多少可以弥补一下维修成本过高的损失。

Though it's not quite profitable to sell consumables, it can make up some of the losses due to the high maintenance cost.

“多少”，副词，表示或多或少，但是肯定有。可以重叠为“多多少少”，作状语，修饰动词。例如：

“多少”, adverb, indicating “some”, “more or less”. Another form is “多多少少”, adverbial, modifying the verb. For example:

（1）这句话多少有点道理。

The saying more or less makes some sense.

（2）这件事我多多少少知道一点儿。

I know a little bit about it.

（3）经过一个月的学习，他们的汉语水平多少有了一些提高。

After a month of studying, their Chinese has more or less improved.

附录

公开招标流程图

成立招标委员会

制定标底

↓

发布招标公告

↓

确定书面投标意向

递交相关材料

↓

资格预审

↓

投标

↓

开标

↓

竞标——评标

↓

定标

↓

商谈合同条款

↓

签订合同

练习
Exercises

一、跟读生词并且纠音。
Read the new words after the teacher and correct your pronunciation.

二、跟读课文并且纠音。
Read the text after the teacher and correct your pronunciation.

三、学生分组，分角色朗读课文一、二。
Divide the students into groups and read the texts 1 & 2 in different roles.

四、学生分组，不看书分角色表演课文一、二。
Divide the students into groups and role play the texts 1 & 2 without referring to the book.

五、角色扮演。(提示：角色可以互换。)
Role play (Note: The roles can be exchanged.)

1. 两人一组，A、B两个角色。**按照下面的要求对话：**
   A：看了招标公告在犹豫要不要参与。担心竞争激烈、手续复杂，等等。
   B：询问A担心什么？有哪些手续和需要递交的文件？

2. 两人一组，A、B两个角色。A的公司中标以后，
   A：感谢B的鼓励；说出中标后的问题——利润少。
   B：询问中标后的问题？帮助A分析怎么样能够获得更大的利润。

六、替换练习。
Substitution drills.

1. 怎么 + 这么长时间才开门， 我还以为 + 你不在家呢。

你	还在上班	你去休假了呢
他	一个人生活呀	他早结婚了呢
	还在谈判呀	签完协议了呢

2．我说什么 ＋ 来着，＋ 大胆尝试，这不就成功了。
前几天他还和我一起吃饭 怎么今天就联系不上了
你还记得老板曾跟我们说什么 不能只顾眼前利益
我上次去他家还见过他的女朋友 怎么现在分手了

3．……， ＋ 多亏你鼓励我。
我考了HSK6级 你给我辅导
我们顺利地签了合同 前期准备工作做得好
小王迷路了 警察帮助了他

4．…… ＋ 由 ＋ 你们公司 ＋ 负责提供耗材……
这份调查报告 比尔 来写
今晚的会议 马莉 主持
这件事 人力资源部 负责

5．看来还是 ＋ 你有经济头脑。
年轻人能干
老板想得远
夏天去那儿旅游比较好

6．咱们别光顾 ＋ 说话，＋ 咱们喝酒 ＋ 吧。
你 让别人吃 你自己也吃
大家 聊天 赶快动身
小王你 做生意 好好放松放松

七、把下面的词语组成句子。
Make a sentence with the following words in each group.

课文一：

1. 招标 入迷 什么 公告 你 让 这么

2. 我 投标 提出 的 想 公司 建议 明天 向

3. 意向 的 有 递交 投标 起码 百 家 书面 就 上

4. 了　资格　来　预审　完　最多　20　家　剩下

5. 也　的　公司　不　有　把握　其它　一定　十足　的

6. 就　只要　拿　着手　准备　主意　了　定　可以

课文一：

1. 有　看来　公司　还是　很　的　你们　实力

2. 比较　签　签　了　就是　倒是　有些　条款　苛刻

3. 外乎　产品　客户　售后服务　不　是　的　质量　和　看重　就

4. 力量　是　的　维修　不　问题　吗　你们　没

5. 为了　公司　的　报价　竞争力　压　我们　把　最　有　价格　让　得　很低

6. 多　由　提供　耗材　的话　公司　就　可以　赚　一些　你们　负责

八、完成句子。

Complete the sentences.

1. 我们学校的留学生非常多，＿＿＿＿＿＿＿＿＿＿＿＿。　（起码）
2. 如果你有什么电脑方面的问题，＿＿＿＿＿＿＿＿＿＿＿＿。　（不妨）
3. ＿＿＿＿＿＿＿＿，要不然我的计划书不会写得这么顺利。（多亏）
4. 这家公司的待遇好倒是好，＿＿＿＿＿＿＿＿＿＿＿＿。　（就是）
5. 这些钱虽然不太多，可是＿＿＿＿＿＿＿＿＿＿＿＿。　（多少）

九、完成对话。

Complete the dialogues.

1. A：天气这么热，我们别加班了吧。
   B：这倒是，＿＿＿＿＿＿＿＿＿＿＿＿＿＿＿＿。　（不过）

2. A：最近怎么没看到小刘？
   B：________________________________。（……着呢）
3. A：马上就要期末考试了吧？
   B：是呀，____________________________。（着手）
4. A：去外企应聘挺难的吧？
   B：________________________________。（不外乎）
5. A：你怎么不和张老师打招呼？
   B：________________________________。（光顾）

十、根据课文的内容填空。
Fill the blanks according to the dialogues in the texts.

齐　远：是呀，竞争这么____________，我能不担心吗？

比　尔：这倒是，不过，你们______________试一下。其他的公司也不一定有____________的把握。

齐　远：你说得有道理，我们是应该试一下。

比　尔：____________的准备工作麻烦吗？

齐　远：不算太麻烦，就是要准备一些投标的文件，你看，这个公告上说：投标人要____________营业执照副本、税务____________副本、____________代表人证明书或授权委托书……

比　尔：还有，近几年的____________报告、银行资信证明等文件以及专业技术人员等信息，……

齐　远：只有通过__________委员会的预审，我们才能获得参与投标的____________。

十一、复述课文二。
Retell the text 2.

十二、完成任务。
Complete the following tasks.

你了解中国的招投标程序吗？可以参看附录。然后，几个人一组，请你们上网查找一个在中国招投标的案例，几个人分析它的过程，从开始到结束，是怎么做的？是否成功？为什么能成功？不成功为什么？分析清楚后，请编排一个情景对话到课堂上来展示这个过程。

Unit 4

第四单元

Shāngwù dàilǐ

商务代理

Business Agent

课文一

Wǒmen shì hěn yǒu shílì de dàilǐshāng

我们是很有实力的代理商

Àimǎ fúzhuāng gōngsī xiǎng zài Běijīng xúnzhǎo dújiā dàilǐshāng. Hóngtú gōngsī de Zhāng zǒng jīnglǐ zhèngzài zhǔchí huìyì, shāngliang zhēngqǔ dédào Àimǎ gōngsī dàilǐquán de shì.

爱玛服装公司想在北京寻找独家代理商。宏图公司的张总经理正在主持会议，商量争取得到爱玛公司代理权的事。

Zhāng zǒng: Wǒmen gōngsī duì Àimǎ gōngsī zài Zhōngguó Běijīng de dújiā dàilǐquán fēicháng gǎn xìngqù. Jīntiān qǐng dàjiā lái, jiùshì yào shāngliang rúhé cái néng dédào zhège dàilǐquán, qǐng tántan nǐmen de xiǎngfǎ.

张　总：我们公司对爱玛公司在中国北京的**独家代理权**非常感兴趣。今天请大家来，就是要商量如何才能得到这个代理权，请谈谈你们的想法。

Gōngguān jīnglǐ: Wǒ rènwéi,wǒmen shì hěn yǒu shílì de dàilǐshāng.

公关经理：我认为，我们是很有**实力**的代理商。

Zhāng zǒng: Duì,shílì fēicháng zhòngyào. Búguò,wèile néng shùnlì ná dào zhège dàilǐquán,wǒmen háishì yào rènzhēn de zuòzuo gōngkè.

张　总：对，实力非常重要。不过，为了能顺利拿到这个代理权，我们还是要认真地做做功课。

Xiāoshòu jīnglǐ: Wǒ kàn guò Àimǎ gōngsī de chǎnpǐn mùlù,juéde zhèxiē chǎnpǐn de yàngshì hé yánsè dōu fēicháng shìhé Běijīng de xiāofèizhě.

销售经理：我看过爱玛公司的产品目录，觉得这些产品的样式和颜色都非常适合北京的消费者。

Gōngguān jīnglǐ: Zánmen zài Běijīng de fúzhuāng hángyè zhōng shì shǔyīshǔèr de,duì Běijīng de fúzhuāng shìchǎng fēicháng liáojiě. Zhè shì zánmen de qiángxiàng.

公关经理：咱们在北京的服装行业中是数一数二的，对北京的服装市场非常了解。这是咱们的**强项**。

Zhāng zǒng: Búguò,mùqián quánqiú jīngjì bù jǐngqì a. Nǐmen de shìchǎng diàochá zuò de zěnmeyàng?

张　总：不过，目前全球经济不**景气**啊。你们的市场调查做得怎么样？

Xiāoshòu jīnglǐ: Zhāng zǒng, diàochá de jiéguǒ shì,Běijīngrén de fúzhuāng gòumǎilì réngrán hěn qiáng,shòu jīnróng wēijī de chōngjī bú shì tèbié dà.

销售经理：张总，调查的结果是，北京人的服装购买力**仍然**很强，受金融危机的**冲击**不是特别大。

Gōngguān jīnglǐ: Zhǐyào yǒu hǎo de xiāoshòu qúdào,zánmen jiù kěyǐ zài Běijīng fúzhuāng shìchǎng shàng fēn yì bēi gēng.

公关经理：只要有好的销售渠道，咱们就可以在北京服装市场上分一杯羹。

Zhāng zǒng: Duì,guānjiàn shì xiāoshòu qúdào. Guówài de gōngsī zhǎo dàilǐshāng shí zuì zhùzhòng zhè yì diǎn.

张　总：对，**关键**是销售渠道。国外的公司找代理商时最**注重**这一点。

Xiāoshòu jīnglǐ: Zhè yì diǎn méi wèntí,zánmen gōngsī yǒu fēngfù de xiāoshòu jīngyàn hé chàngtōng de xiāoshòu qúdào. Zánmen de yíngxiāo wǎngluò biànbù Běijīng de gè dà gòuwù zhōngxīn.
销售经理：这一点没问题，咱们公司有丰富的销售经验和**畅通**的销售渠道。咱们的营销**网络遍布**北京的各大**购物中心**。

Gōngguān jīnglǐ: Háiyǒu zánmen dàilǐ de yèwù dàduō shì zhēnduì gāoduān kèhù de,zài gāoduān kèhùqún zhōng zhīmíngdù hěn gāo, zhè hé Àimǎ gōngsī de shìchǎng dìngwèi hěn xiāngfú.
公关经理：还有，咱们代理的业务大多是**针对高端**客户的，在高端**客户群**中知名度很高，这和爱玛公司的市场**定位**很相符。

Xiāoshòu jīnglǐ: Shì de,tāmen de chǎnpǐn bù guāng zài Yìdàlì hěn yǒumíng, zài Ōuzhōu de qítā guójiā yě hěn chàngxiāo,kěyǐ shuō tāmen de fúzhuāng yǐnlǐng le Ōuzhōu de shíshàng.
销售经理：是的，他们的产品不光在意大利很有名，在欧洲的其他国家也很**畅销**，可以说他们的服装**引领**了欧洲的**时尚**。

Zhāng zǒng: Zhè yě shì wǒ kànhǎo tāmen chǎnpǐn de yuányīn.
张　总：这也是我看好他们产品的原因。

Xiāoshòu jīnglǐ: Wǒmen gōngsī rúguǒ néng nádào zhège dàilǐquán,wǒmen de yèwù kěndìng huì gèng shàng yì céng lóu.
销售经理：我们公司如果能拿到这个代理权，我们的业务肯定会更上一层楼的。

Zhāng zǒng: Nà hái yòng shuō,dàjiā zài tǎolùn yíxià hái yǒu shémen wèntí.
张　总：那还用说，大家再讨论一下还有什么问题。

Xiāoshòu jīnglǐ: Zhāng zǒng, zài xià zhōusān zhīqián wǒmen huì zuò chū yí fèn xiángxì de dàilǐ fāng'àn.
销售经理：张总，在下周三之前我们会做出一份详细的代理方案。

Text 1

We are a very competitive agent

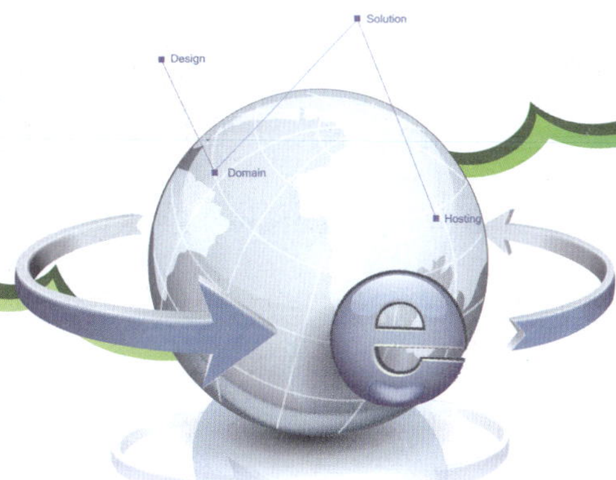

Emma Garment Company intends to find an exclusive agent in Beijing. Mr. Zhang, general manager of Hongtu Company, is presiding a meeting, discussing the plans to acquire the exclusive agency of Emma Garment.

Zhang: We are very interested to be the exclusive agent for Emma Garment in Beijing. Today we meet here to discuss how we can acquire the exclusive agency; please express your opinions.

PR Manager: I think we are a very competitive agent.

Zhang: Yes, strength is very important. However, in order to be successful, we still need to do our homework.

Sales Manager: I have seen the Emma Company's samples catalogue. The design and color of the products fit the Beijing consumers.

PR Manager: We are either No. 1 or No. 2 in Beijing's garment industry, and very familiar with the garment market here. That's our advantage.

Zhang: But the global economy is still sluggish. How is your market research going?

Sales Manager: Mr. Zhang, the results of the market research indicate that the garment purchasing power of Beijingers is still strong, and not much impacted by the financial crisis.

PR Manager: As long as we have good sales channels, we can get our share in Beijing's garment market.

Zhang: Right, the sales channel is the key that foreign companies are most concerned with when they look for an agent.

Sales Manager: No problem. Our company has rich sales experiences and unimpeded sales channels. And our sales networks are all over the shopping centers in Beijing.

PR Manager: Besides, the business for which we act as agent mostly caters to high-end customers, and our company is well-known among high-end customer groups, and that goes along the market orientation of Emma Company.

Sales Manager: Yes, their products are not only famous in Italy but sell very well in other European countries. We might as well say their garments lead the fashion of Europe.

Zhang: That's why I preferred their products in the first place.

Sales Manager: If our company get the agency, our business will sure step onto a higher plateau.

Zhang: That's for sure. Now let's discuss whether there are any other questions.

Sales Manager: Mr. Zhang, we will come up with a detailed plan for the agency before next Wednesday.

生词 New words

1	独家	dújiā	exclusive
2	代理权	dàilǐquán	agency
3	实力	shílì	competitive
4	强项	qiángxiàng	advantage
5	景气	jǐngqì	prosperity
6	仍然	réngrán	still
7	冲击	chōngjī	to lash
8	关键	guānjiàn	crux,key
9	注重	zhùzhòng	to concern with
10	畅通	chàngtōng	unimpeded
11	网络	wǎngluò	networks
12	遍布	biànbù	to spread all over

13	购物中心	gòuwùzhōngxīn	shopping centre
14	针对	zhēnduì	cater to
15	高端	gāoduān	high-end
16	客户群	kèhùqún	client group
17	定位	dìngwèi	orientation
18	畅销	chàngxiāo	to sell well
19	引领	yǐnlíng	to lead
20	时尚	shíshàng	fashion

专有名词 Proper nouns

宏图公司
Hóngtú Gōngsī
Hongtu Company

注释 Notes

1. 为了能顺利拿到这个代理权，我们还要认真地做做功课。

In order to get the agency successfully, we still need to do our homework.

“做功课”原来是指学生做作业，这里是说要多做准备。例如：

“做功课”, literally “doing homework”, meaning to make enough preparations. For example:

（1）要想谈判成功，就要在谈判前多做功课。
For successful negotiations, we must do our homework well beforehand.

（2）他事先做了很多功课，才在演讲比赛中获得了第一名。
He had done much homework before he won the first prize in the speech contest.

（3）做足功课是成功的关键。
The key to success is to do enough homework.

2. 我们在北京的服装行业中是数一数二的。

We are either No. 1 or No. 2 in Beijing's garment industry.

"数一数二" 形容很突出，如果排名，那就是在第一、第二名的位置。"数"，动词，是计算起来、比较起来(最突出)的意思。例如：

"数一数二" describes something outstanding, ranking either the first or the second position. "数", verb, meaning "count" or "compare"(with the meaning of the most prominent). For example:

(1) 他的口语水平在我们班是数一数二的。

His oral language level ranks either No.1 or No.2 in our class.

(2) 桂林的风景在中国是数一数二的。

The landscape of Guilin is among the best of China.

(3) 德国生产汽车的水平在世界上是数一数二的。

The auto manufacturing level of Germany is among the top of the world.

3. 只要有好的销售渠道，就可以在北京服装市场上分一杯羹。

As long as we have good sales channels, we can get our share in Beijing's garment market.

"羹", 名词，是指用蒸、煮的方法做出来的糊状食物。"分一杯羹"意思是说努力得到好处。在商业竞争中，指占有市场，获得市场份额。

"羹", noun, referring a paste-like food cooked by steaming boiling. "分一杯羹" means to try to get benefits. In business competition, it refers to occupying the market or getting a market share.

4. 我们的业务肯定会更上一层楼的。

Our business will sure step onto a higher plateau.

唐朝诗人王之涣的诗《登鹳雀楼》中有:"欲穷千里目，更上一层楼"。后来用"更上一层楼"比喻再提高一步。

The Tang poet Wang Zhihuan wrote in his *Ascending the Guanque Tower,* "If you desire a grander sight, ascend to a greater height." Later , "更上一层楼" is used to mean "one step further in progress".

课文二

Wǒmen tán yíxià dàilǐ xiéyì de jùtǐ shìyí

我们谈一下代理协议的具体事宜

Àimǎ gōngsī de jīnglǐ Mǎ Lì kàn le jǐ jiā gōngsī de dàilǐ fāng'àn hòu,duì Hóngtú gōngsī de zuì mǎnyì.Gōngsī kāi huì yánjiū hòu,juédìng bǎ zài Běijīng de dújiā dàilǐquán jiāo gěi Hóngtú gōngsī.Jīntiān, Mǎ Lì yuē Zhāng zǒng lái,jìn yí bù qiàtán dàilǐ xiéyì de jùtǐ shìyí.

爱玛公司的经理马莉看了几家公司的代理方案后,对宏图公司的最满意。公司开会研究后，决定把在北京的独家代理权交给宏图公司。今天，马莉约张总来，进一步洽谈代理协议的具体事宜。

Mǎ Lì: Wǒ zǐxì kàn le guì gōngsī de jìhuàshū. Jīntiān qǐng nín lái,jiù shì xiǎng hé nín tán yíxià dàilǐ xiéyì de jùtǐ shìyí.

马　莉：我仔细看了贵公司的计划书。今天请您来，就是想和您谈一下代理协议的具体**事宜**。

Zhāng zǒng: Hǎo de,wǒ xiǎng xiān tīngting nín de xiǎngfǎ.

张　总：好的，我想先听听您的想法。

Mǎ Lì: Wǒ xiǎng zánmen xiān bǎ xiāoshòu dìng'é dìng xiàlai.

马　莉：我想咱们先把销售**定额**定下来。

Zhāng zǒng: Bù zhī nín zhùyì dào méiyǒu?Wǒmen zài dàilǐ fāng'àn lǐ jiànyì guì gōngsī shìdàng de xiàtiáo shìchǎng cānkǎojià,kěnéng gèng lìyú nǐmen chǎnpǐn dǎ rù Běijīng shìchǎng.

张　总：不知您注意到没有？我们在代理方案里建议贵公司适当地**下调**市场**参考价**，可能更利于你们的产品打入北京市场。

Mǎ Lì: Nǐmen Zhōngguórén bú shì cháng shuō"yì fēn qián,yì fēn huò"ma? Wǒmen de chǎnpǐn zhìliàng、shíshàngxìng dōu méideshuō, zhèxiē jiàgé shì bǐjiào hélǐ de.

马　莉：你们中国人不是常说"一分钱一分货"吗？我们的产品质量、时尚性都没得说，这些价格是比较合理的。

Zhāng zǒng: Zhèyàng de huà,nín zhīqián tí chū de xiāoshòu dìng'é wǒmen jiù hěn nán wánchéng le.

张　总：这样的话，您之前提出的销售定额我们就很难完成了。

Mǎ Lì: "Àimǎ"shì guójì pǐnpái,xiāoshòu yīnggāi bù chéng wèntí.

马　莉："爱玛"是国际品牌，销售应该不成问题。

Zhāng zǒng: Dàn tā shì chūcì jìnrù Běijīng shìchǎng. Gēnjù wǒmen de shìchǎng diàoyán bàogào,Běijīng de xiāofèizhě duì zhège pǐnpái de jiēshòudù hái hěn dī.

张　总：但它是**初次**进入北京市场。根据我们的市场调研报告，北京的消费者对这个品牌的**接受度**还很低。

Mǎ Lì: Wǒmen huì kǎolǜ zhège qíngkuàng de, érqiě wánchéng rènwù hòu wǒmen huì gěi dàilǐ shāng yídìng de jiǎnglì zuòwéi huíbào, bǐrú shíwù jiǎnglì、lǚyóu děngdeng.

马　莉：我们会考虑这个情况的，而且完成任务后我们会给代理商一定的奖励作为回报，比如实物奖励、旅游等等。

Zhāng zǒng: Fúzhuāng xiāoshòu yǒu hěn qiáng de jìjiéxìng, guì gōngsī zài quèdìng xiāoshòu dìng'é shí shì bu shì yīnggāi kǎolǜ yíxià zhège yīnsù?

张　总：服装销售有很强的季节性，贵公司在确定销售定额时是不是还应该考虑一下这个**因素**？

Mǎ Lì: Wǒmen dāngrán kǎolǜ dào le jiàngjià yīnsù. Dànshì yīnwèi wǒmen de chǎnpǐn shì dà pǐnpái,suǒyǐ jiàngjià de fúdù bú huì tài dà.

马　莉：我们当然考虑到了**降价**因素。但是因为我们的产品是大品牌，所以降价的**幅度**不会太大。

Zhāng zǒng: Nà nǐmen néngfǒu duì xiāoshòu dìng'é zuò yìxiē tiáozhěng?

张　总：那你们能否对销售定额作一些调整？

Mǎ Lì: Zhīqián tí chū de yí gè jìdù de xiāoshòu dìng'é shì yìbǎi liùshí wàn yuán rénmínbì, kǎolǜ qiánmiàn de zhèxiē yīnsù,wǒmen kě jiàng dào yìbǎi wǔshí wàn yuán rénmínbì. Rúguǒ wánchéng dìng'é,wǒmen huì zhīfù bǎi fēn zhī wǔ de yòngjīn.

马　莉：之前提出的一个季度的销售定额是160万元人民币，考虑前面的这些因素，我们可降到150万元人民币。如果完成定额，我们会支付5%的**佣金**。

Zhāng zǒng: Tōngcháng wǒmen de yòngjīn dōu zài bǎi fēn zhī shí zuǒyòu,érqiě "Àimǎ"zài Běijīng hái méiyǒu zhīmíngdù,wǒmen kāituò shìchǎng shí,xuānchuán tuīguǎng de chéngběn fēicháng gāo.

张　总：通常我们的佣金都在10%左右,而且"爱玛"在北京还没有**知名度**，我们**开拓**市场时，**宣传**推广的成本非常高。

Mǎ Lì: Nǐ shuō de yě yǒu dàolǐ,dànshì bǎi fēn zhī shí de yòngjīn tài gāo le. Zhèyàngba,wánchéng xiāoshòu dìng'é hòu,měi xiāoshòu shí wàn yuán,yòngjīn tígāo líng diǎn wǔ ge bǎifēndiǎn,zuì gāo bù chāoguò bǎi fēn zhī bā.

马　莉：你说的也有道理，但是10%的佣金太高了。这样吧，完成销售定额后，每销售10万元，佣金提高0.5个**百分点**，最高不超过8%。

Zhāng zǒng: Nàme yòngjīn rúhé zhīfù?

张　总：那么佣金如何支付？

Mǎ Lì: Wǒmen kěyǐ zhíjiē cóng fāpiào jīn'é zhōng kòuchú.

马　莉：我们可以直接从发票**金额**中扣除。

Zhāng zǒng: Kěyǐ.

张　总：可以。

Mǎ Lì: Nǐmen měi sān ge yuè yào xiàng wǒmen tígōng yí cì yǒuguān shìchǎng hángqíng hé yònghù yìjiàn de xiángxì bàogào,fāngbiàn wǒmen jíshí liáojiě qíngkuàng.

马　莉：你们每三个月要向我们提供一次有关市场行情和用户意见的详细报告，**方便**我们**及时**了解情况。

Zhāng zǒng: Méiwèntí.

张　总：没问题。

Mǎ Lì: Háiyǒu,wǒmen duì cuànhuò de chǔfá shì fēicháng yángé de,qíngkuàng yánzhòng de,wǒmen huì shōuhuí dàilǐquán.

马　莉：还有，我们对窜货的**处罚**是非常严格的，情况严重的，我们会收回代理权。

Zhāng zǒng: Nín fàngxīn, wǒmen shì bú huì ràng zhèzhǒng qíngkuàng fāshēng de. Háiyǒu yì diǎn,mùqián gè dà shāngchǎng duìyú xīn pǐnpái de jìnchǎng dōu shèlì le yídìng shù'é de huòwù shàngjiàfèi huò jìnchǎngfèi,érqiě shùmù rìyì shàngzhǎng,cóng jǐ qiān yuán dào jǐ wàn yuán bù děng. Zài zhè fāngmiàn,xīwàng nénggòu dédào guì gōngsī de zhīchí,jǐyǔ bàoxiāo.

张　总：您放心，我们是不会让这种情况发生的。还有一点，目前各大商场对于新品牌的进场都设立了一定数额的货物上架费或进场费，而且数目**日益上涨**，从几千元到几万元不等。在这方面，希望能够得到贵公司的支持，给予**报销**。

Mǎ Lì: Wǒmen yǒu xiāngguān de zhīchí. Jīntiān jiù tán dào zhèr ba.Dàilǐ xiéyì zhǔnbèi hǎo yǐhòu,wǒmen zài gēn nín liánxì.

马　莉：我们有相关的支持。今天就谈到这儿吧。代理协议准备好以后，我们再跟您联系。

Zhāng zǒng: Hǎo de,wǒmen děng nín de xiāoxi.

张　总：好的，我们等您的消息。

Text 2

Let's discuss the details of the agent agreement

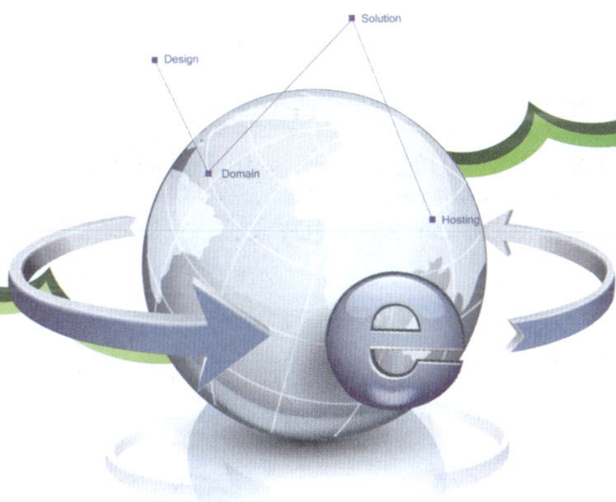

Maria General manager of Emma Company, reads the agency plans of several companies and is most satisfied with the one of Hongtu Company. After discussions the company decides to award the exclusive agency to Hongtu Company. Today, Maria makes an appointment with Mr. Zhang for further talks on the details of the agent agreement.

Maria: I have carefully studied the plan of your company. Today we invite you here to discuss the details of the agent agreement.

Zhang: OK, I'd like to hear your opinion.

Maria: I think we should first of all set the sales quota.

Zhang: I don't know whether you have noticed that we proposed in our plan for your company to lower your reference prices. I think that will better enable your products to penetrate the Beijing market.

Maria: Don't you Chinese often say "one cent of money is worth one cent of value"? The quality and trendiness of our products are unquestionable, so the prices are quite reasonable.

Zhang: In that case, it is very difficult for us to complete the sales quota you proposed before.

Maria: "Emma" is an international brand and there won't be any problem in the sales.

Zhang: But it's the first time we sell the product in the Beijing market. According to our market research report, the consumers in Beijing haven't accepted the brand well enough.

Maria: We will take that into consideration. And if the task is accomplished, we will award the agent some kind of prize, such as material prize or travel etc.

Zhang: The sales of garments vary with the change of seasons. Don't you think you should take that into consideration?

Maria: Of course we considered the factor of price reduction. But our products are of big brands, so the reduction of prices won't be substantial.

Zhang: Can you adjust the sales quota then?

Maria: The sales quota for a season we proposed is 1.6 million RMB Yuan; considering the above-mentioned factors, we may lower it to 1.5 million. If the quota is completed, we will pay a 5% commission.

Zhang: Usually our commission is around 10%. And "Emma" is not yet known to the consumers, so the publicity cost will be pretty high when we do the marketing.

Maria: What you said is reasonable, but a 10% commission is too high. OK then, after the sales quota is completed, the commission will increase by 0.5 percent for every 100,000 Yuan of additional sales revenue, with 8% as the upper limit.

Zhang: How would you pay the commission?

Maria: We can directly deduct it from the invoice amount.

Zhang: OK.

Maria: You're supposed to provide us a detailed report on the market conditions and customers' feedback so as to keep us informed of the latest developments.

Zhang: No problem.

Maria: Moreover, we maintain a strict fine for cross-regional sales; for serious cases we shall withdraw the agency rights.

Zhang: Just rest assured, we won't allow that to happen. One more thing, now the big shopping centers all set a shelf-space fee or entry fee, which are always on the rise, ranging from a few thousands to tens of thousands. We wish to have your support of reimbursement in this respect.

Maria: We do have relevant support. Let's call it a day here. We will contact you when the agency agreement is ready.

Zhang: OK, we will wait for the good news from you.

生词 New words

1	进一步	jìnyíbù	go a step further
2	洽谈	qiàtán	to consult
3	事宜	shìyí	matters concerned
4	定额	dìng'é	quota
5	下调	xiàtiáo	to lower

6	参考	cānkǎo	to refer to
7	初次	chūcì	the first time
8	接受度	jiēshòudù	acceptance
9	因素	yīnsù	factor
10	降价	jiàngjià	to reduce the prices
11	幅度	fúdù	range
12	佣金	yòngjīn	commission
13	知名度	zhīmíngdù	popularity
14	开拓	kāituò	to open up
15	宣传	xuānchuán	publicity
16	百分点	bǎifēndiǎn	percentage
17	金额	jīn'é	amount of money
18	方便	fāngbiàn	to make convenient for
19	及时	jíshí	in time
20	处罚	chǔfá	to punish
21	日益	rìyì	day by day
22	上涨	shàngzhǎng	to rise
23	报销	bàoxiāo	to reimburse

专有名词 Proper nouns

1. 你们中国人不是常说"一分钱一分货"吗，我觉得这句话很有道理。

Don't you Chinese often say "one cent of money is worth one cent of value"? I think that makes sense.

"一分钱一分货"是俗语，指商品的价格与质量成正比，质量好的东西价格会贵一些。

"一分钱一分货" is a popular saying, indicating the price of a commodity corresponds to its quality, and things of higher quality will be more expensive.

2. 我们产品的质量、时尚性都没得说。

The quality and trendiness of our products are unquestionable.

"没得说"常用在口语中，表示很好，好得不用说了。例如：

"没得说", usually used in spoken Chinese, indicating very good, good to the point that no comment is necessary.

（1）我们俩的关系没得说。

Our relationship is great.

（2）他的汉语没得说。

His Chinese is excellent.

（3）他这个人对待别人没得说。

He is always good to others.

3. 北京的消费者对这个品牌的接受度还很低，而且“爱玛”在北京还没有知名度，……

The consumers in Beijing have not yet quite accepted this brand, and "Emma" is not yet known to them,...

“接受度、知名度”是指人或事物被社会公众认可、熟悉的程度。“度”表示程度。例如：

“接受度、知名度” refers to the degree in which a person or event is accepted by the public. “度” is the degree. For example:

（1）我们只有研究中国人的习俗，才能设计出接受度高的产品。

Only by studying the customs of the Chinese can we design the products of acceptability.

（2）这位中国女演员在欧洲的知名度比在国内高。

The Chinese actress is more well-known in Europe than in China.

（3）这次市场调查的结果准确度不高。

The findings of the market research are not very accurate.

4. 我们的窜货处罚是非常严格的，情况严重的，我们会收回代理权。

We maintain a strict fine for cross-regional sales; for serious cases we shall withdraw the agency.

在代理业务中，有时会发生窜货现象。这种现象是，经销网络中的各级代理商、分公司等为了自己的利益，跨区域销售所经销的产品，造成市场秩序混乱，从而使其他经销商对产品失去信心，消费者对品牌失去信任。对于这种现象，厂商的处罚有罚款等。如果多次发生这种现象，代理商的代理权就保不住了。

In the agent operations, the phenomenon of cross-regional sale sometimes takes place. For their own interests, the agents or subsidiaries at different levels sell a product beyond the designated region, causing a disorder of the market; therefore other dealers may lose their confidence in the product and consumers lose their trust in the brand. The manufacturer usually levies a fine on that. Repetitive happenings of such a phenomenon may deprive an agent of the right of agency.

附录

销售代理协议

合同号：

日　期：

为在**平等**（píngděng, equality）**互利**（hùlì, mutual benefit）的基础上发展贸易，有关方按**下列**（xiàliè, as follows）**条件**（tiáojiàn, conditions）签订本协议：

一、订约人：

供货人（以下称**甲方**jiǎfāng, party A）：

销售代理人（以下称**乙方**yǐfāng, party B）：

甲方委托乙方为销售代理人，推销下列商品。

二、商品名称及数量或金额：

双方约定，乙方在协议有效期内，销售不少于_____的商品。

三、经销地区：

只限在_____地区。

四、订单的确认：

本协议所规定商品的数量、价格及装运条件等，应在每笔交易中确认，其**细目**（xìmù, particulars）应在双方签订的销售协议书中作出规定。

五、付款：

订单确认之后，乙方须按照有关确认书所规定的时间，开立以甲方为受益人的保兑的、不可撤销的即期信用证。乙方开出信用证后，应立即通知甲方，以便甲方准备交货。

六、佣金：

在本协议期满时，**若**（ruò,if）乙方完成了第二款所规定的数额，甲方应按装运货物所收到的发票**累计**（lěijì, to aggregate）总金额付给乙方___%的佣金。

七、市场情况报告：

乙方每3个月向甲方提供一次有关当时市场情况和用户意见的详细报告。同时，乙方应随时向甲方提供其他供应商的**类似**（lèisì, similar）商品样品及其价格、销售情况和广告资料。

八、宣传广告费用：

在本协议有效期内，乙方在**上述**（shàngshù, mentioned above）经销地区所作广告宣传的**一切**（yíqiè, all）费用，由乙方自理。乙方须事先向甲方提供宣传广告的图案及文字说明，由甲方**审阅**（shěnyuè, examine carefully and critically）同意。

九、协议有效期：

本协议经双方签字后**生效**（shēngxiào, to go into effect），有效期为_____天，自_______至_______。若一方希望**延长**（yáncháng, to extend）本协议，则须在本协议期满前1个月书面通知另一方，经双方协商决定。

若协议一方**未**（wèi, have not）**履行**（lǚxíng, to implement）协议条款，另一方有权**终止**（zhōngzhǐ,to terminate）协议。

十、仲裁（zhòngcái, Arbitration）：

在履行协议过程中，如产生**争议**（zhēngyì, disputes），双方应友好协商解决。若通过友好协商达不成协议，则**提交**（tíjiāo, to submit）**中国国际贸易促进**

委员会对外贸易仲裁委员会（Zhōngguó guójì màoyì cùjìn wěiyuánhuì duìwài màoyì zhòngcái wěiyuánhuì, the Foreign Trade Arbitration Commission of the China Council for the Promotion of International Trade），根据**该**(gāi, this)会仲裁**程序**（chéngxù, procedure）**暂行**（zànxíng, provisional）规定进行仲裁。该委员会的决定是**终局**（zhōngjú, final）的，对双方**均**（jūn, both, all）具有**约束**(yūeshù, bind)力。仲裁费用，除另有规定外，由**败诉方**（bàisùfāng, the losing party）负担。

十一、其他条款：

1. 甲方不得向经销地区其他买主供应本协议所规定的商品。如有询价，当**转达**(zhuǎndá, to pass on)给乙方洽办。若有买主希望从甲方**直接**(zhíjiē, direct)订购，甲方可以供货，但甲方须**将**(jiāng, used to shift the object to before the verb)有关销售确认书副本寄给乙方，并按所达成交易的发票金额**给予**(jǐyǔ, to give)乙方_____%的佣金。

2. 若乙方在____月内未能向甲方提供**至少**(zhìshǎo, a minimum of)________订货，甲方不**承担**(chéngdān, to undertake)本协议的**义务**(yìwù, obligation)。

3. 对双方政府间的贸易，甲方有权按其政府的**授权**(shòuquán, to grant)进行有关的直接贸易，而不受本协议约束。乙方不得**干涉**(gānshè, to interfere in)此种直接贸易，也无权向甲方提出**任何**(rènhé, any)**补偿**(bǔcháng,compensation)或佣金要求。

4. 本协议受签约双方所签订的销售确认条款的**制约**(zhìyuē, to subject to)。

本协议于______年___月___日在______签订，**正本**(zhèngběn, originals)两份，甲、乙双方各**执**(zhí, to hold)一份。

甲方：　　　　　　　　　　　　　　　　乙方：

（签字qiānzì, signature）　　　　　　　（签字）

（摘自中国贸易网）

Appendix

Sales Agency Agreement

No：

Date：

This Agreement is entered into between the parties concerned on the basis of equality and mutual benefit to develop business on terms and conditions mutually agreed upon as follows:

1. Contracting Parties

Supplier:（hereinafter called"party A"）

Agent:（hereinafter called"party B"）

Party A hereby appoint Party B to act as his selling agent to sell the commodity mentioned below.

2. Commodity and Quantity or Amount

It is mutually agreed that Party B shall undertake to sell not less than... of the aforesaid commodity in the duration of this Agreement。

3. Territory

In ... Only.

4. Confirmation of Orders

The quantities, prices and shipments of the commodities stated in this Agreement shall be confirmed in each transaction, the particulars of which are to be specified in the Sales Confirmation signed by the two parties hereto.

5. Payment

After confirmation of the order, Party B shall arrange to open a confirmed, irrevocable L/C available by draft at sight in favour of Party A within the time stipulated in the relevant S/C. Party B shall also notify Party A immediately after L/C is opened so that Party A can get prepared for delivery.

6. Commission

Upon the expiration of the Agreement and Party B's fullfilment of the total turnover mentioned in Article 2, Party A shall pay to Party B... % commission on the basis of the aggregate amount of the invoice value against the shipments effected.

7. Reports on Market Conditions

Party B shall forward once every three months to party A detailed reports on current market conditions and of consumers' comments. Meanwhile, Party B shall,from time to time, send to party A samples of similar commodities offered by other suppliers, together with their prices, sales information and advertising materials.

8. Advertising & Publicity Expenses

Party B shall bear all expenses for advertising and publicity within the aforementioned territory in the duration of this Agreement and submit to Party A all patterns and/or drawings and description for prior approval.

9. Validity of Agreement

This Agreement, after its being signed by the parties concerned, shall remain in force for... days from ... to ... If either Party wishes to extend this Agreement, he shall notice, in writing, the other party one month prior to its expiration. The matter shall be decided by the agreement and by consent of the parties hereto. Should either party fail to implement the terms and conditions herein, the other party is entitled to terminate this Agreement.

10. Arbitration

All disputes arising from the execution of this Agreement shall be settled through friendly consultations. In case no settlement can be reached, the case in dispute shall then be submitted to the Foreign Trade Arbitration Commission of the China Council for the Promotion of International Trade for arbitration in accordance with its provisional rules of procedure. The decision made by this Commission shall be regarded as final and binding upon both parties. Arbitration fees shall be borne by the losing party ,unless otherwise awarded.

11. Other Terms & Conditions

(1) Party A shall not supply the contracted commodity to any other buyer(s) in the above mentioned territory. Direct enquiries, if any, will be referred to Party B. However, should any other buyers wish to deal with Party A directly, Party A may do so. But party A shall send to Party B a copy of Sales Confirmation and give Party B...% commission on the basis of the net invoice value of the transaction(s)concluded.

(2)Should Party B fail to pass on his orders to Party A in a period of ... months for a minimum of ..., Party A shall not bind himself to this Agreement.

(3)For any business transacted between governments of both Parties, Party A may handle such direct dealings as authorized by Party A's government without binding himself to this Agreement. Party B shall not interfere in such direct dealings nor shall Party B bring forward any demand for compensation therefrom.

(4)This Agreement shall be subject to the terms and conditions in the Sales Confirmation signed by both parties hereto.

This Agreement is signed on ... at... and is in two originals; each Party holds one.

Party A:
(Signature)

Party B:
(Signature)

(http://www.cntrades.com)

练习

Exercises

一、跟读生词并且纠音。

Read the new words after the teacher and correct your pronunciation.

二、跟读课文并且纠音。

Read the text after the teacher and correct your pronunciation.

三、学生分组，分角色朗读课文一、二。

Divide the students into groups and read the texts 1 & 2 in different roles.

四、学生分组，不看书分角色表演课文一、二。

Divide the students into groups and role play the texts 1 & 2 without referring to the book.

五、角色扮演。（提示：角色可以互换。）

Role play (Note: The roles can be exchanged.)

两个学生A和B一组，模拟一个争取独家代理权的洽谈。

内容：中国的汽车公司A想代理德国公司B的汽车配件。

双方要谈到：销售渠道、行业经验、市场推广、广告费用、佣金等。

六、替换练习。

Substitution drills.

1. 我们在北京的服装行业中 + 是数一数二的。

   他的销售业绩在全公司

   小马的游泳水平在同事中

   这种产品的质量在同等产品中

2. 我们代理的业务大多是针对高端客户的，这 +和 + 爱玛公司的市场定位很 + 相符。

你的行为	你的身份
账上的金额	实际营业额
他的言行	年龄

3. **他们的产品 + 不光在意大利很有名，在欧洲的其他国家+ 也+ 很畅销。**

马莉　　很能干　　在朋友中　　有人缘
海尔　　在中国做得很成功　　在海外　　很有名
汽车　　是代步工具　　　　是身份的象征

4. **我们产品的质量、时尚性都　+　没得说。**

小王和老顾客的关系
你的社交能力真是
大品牌的售后服务

5. **你们 + 每 + 三个月 + 要向我们提供一 + 次 + 有关市场行情和用户意见的详细报告。**

小王　　一个星期　　去　　两　　超市
业务员　　两个月　　出差　　一
妈妈　　三天　　给我打　　一　　电话

七、把下面的词语组成句子。

Make a sentence with the following words.

课文一：

1. 商量　这个　如何　才能　代理权　我们　要　得到

2. 代理权　为了　顺利　到　这个　我们　还　做做　能　要　拿　地　功课　认真

3. 北京　服装　仍旧　购买力　很强　人　的

4. 的　公司　国外　注重　找　最　这　一点　代理商　时

5. 的　我们　的　营销　大　北京　各　购物中心　网络　遍布

6. 也　是　这　产品　的　原因　看好　他们　我

课文二：

1. 先　我　定　想　咱们　定额　销售　把　下来

2. 这　打入　北京　可能　利于　的　产品　你们　市场　更

3. 这个　北京　还　很　对　品牌　的　的　消费者　接受度　低

4. 奖励　给　作为　我们　代理商　一定　的　回报　会

5. 不　贵　因素　一下　这个　公司　是　是　考虑　还　应该

6. 对　那　你们　定额　做　一些　能否　调整　销售

7. 从　我们　发票　可以　中　扣除　直接　金额

8. 的　我们　这种　是　不　情况　会　发生　让

八、完成句子。

Complete the sentences.

1. 这件衣服的颜色、款式都______________________。　（适合）
2. 十多年没见张经理了，______________________。　（仍旧）
3. ______________________，我们修改了代理方案。　（针对）
4. 通过努力学习，______________________。　（日益）
5. 超市延长了营业时间，______________________。　（方便，〈动词〉）

九、根据课文的内容填空。

Fill the blanks according to the dialogues in the text.

马　莉：你们中国人不是常说"____________"吗，我觉得这句话很有道理。我们产品的____________、时尚性都____________，这些价格是比较____________的。

张　总：这样的话，您之前提出的销售____________我们就很难完成了。"爱玛"虽然是国际品牌，但是______________进入北京市场。根据我们的市场调研报告，北京的消费者对这个品牌______________还很低。

马　莉：我们会考虑这个情况的，而且______________任务后我们会给代理商一定的奖励作为回报，比如实物奖励、旅游等等。

张　总：服装销售有很______________的季节性，贵公司在确定销售定额时是不是还应该考虑一下这个因素？

马　莉：我们当然考虑到了降价因素。但是因为我们的产品是大品牌，所以降价的______________不会太大。

十、复述课文一。

Retell the text 1.

十一、完成任务。

Complete the following tasks.

（一）假设一家韩国著名的家电公司（冰箱）初次进入中国市场，要在中国南方寻找代理商。厂商为A和代理商为B。请设计一段对话，注意使用课文中学过的词语和句子。

（二）几个人一组，请去网上查找资料，找到一家你们国家（或者任意选择一个国家）的厂商在中国代理的情况，或者是中国的产品在你的国家代理的情况。请你们一起在课堂上向你的老师和同学们介绍你们了解到的情况。

Unit 5

第五单元

Shìchǎng diàoyán

市场调研

Market Research

课文一

Nǐmen gōngsī yě zài zuò shìchǎng diàoyán a

你们公司也在做市场调研啊

Jīntiān，Qí Yuǎn、Zhào Hóng lái Mǎ Lì jiā fǔdǎo tā shāngwù hànyǔ，Bǐ'ěr yě lái le.

今天，齐远、赵红来马莉家辅导她商务汉语，比尔也来了。

Bǐ'ěr: Nǐmen jīntiān xué shénme?
比　尔：你们今天学什么？

Mǎ Lì: Bùrú jiù shuōshuo hé shìchǎng diàoyán yǒuguān de huàtí.
马　莉：不如就说说和市场调研有关的话题。

Zhào Hóng: Hǎo a.
赵　红：好啊。

Bǐ'ěr: Nǐmen gōngsī yě zài zuò shìchǎng diàoyán a. Wǒ yě zhèng máng zhè shìr ne.
比　尔：你们公司在做市场调研啊。我也正忙这事儿呢。

Mǎ Lì: Wǒmen de chǎnpǐn yào jìnrù zhōngguó shìchǎng, dāngrán shǎobuliǎo yào zuò shìchǎng diàoyán, zhījǐzhībǐ ma.
马　莉：我们的产品要进入中国市场，当然少不了要做市场调研，**知己知彼**嘛。

Bǐ'ěr: Duì!Zuò yíngxiāo jiù shì xūyào diàoyán.
比　尔：对！做营销就是需要调研。

Mǎ Lì: Shì a, kēxué kěxíng de yíngxiāo diàoyán jiélùn nénggòu bāngzhù qǐyè zuòchū yìxiē zhòngdà juécè.
马　莉：是啊，**科学**可行的营销调研**结论**能够帮助企业作出一些**重大决策**。

Qí Yuǎn: Xiànzài yǒu hěnduō zhuānyè de diàoyán gōngsī, nǐ kěyǐ qǐng tāmen bāngmáng.
齐　远：现在有很多**专门**的调研公司，你可以请他们帮忙。

Mǎ Lì: Shì de, wǒmen de xiāofèizhě xūqiú shìchǎng diàoyán fāng'àn jiùshì xiàng shèhuì gōngkāi zhāobiāo de.
马　莉：是的，我们的消费者**需求**市场调研方案就是向社会公开招标的。

Bǐ'ěr: Jìnxíng de zěnmeyàng le?
比　尔：进行得怎么样了？

Mǎ Lì: Yǎnxià, yǐjīng yǒu yì jiā Běijīng de qǐhuà gōngsī wèi wǒmen zuò hǎo le yí fèn shìchǎng diàoyán yǔ fēnxī bàogào.
马　莉：**眼下**，已经有一家北京的**企划**公司为我们做好了一份市场调研与分析报告。

Bǐ'ěr: Wěituō biérén zuò. Nǐmen qīngsōng le. Wǒmen gōngsī de děi wǒ zìjǐ zuò.
比　尔：**委托**别人做。你们**轻松**了。我们公司的得我自己做。

Mǎ Lì：Dāngrán le！Nǐ shì zhè fāngmiàn de zhuānjiā ma.
马　莉：当然了！你是这方面的**专家**嘛。

Zhào Hóng: Mǎ Lì，nǐmen de shìchǎng diàoyán yǔ fēnxī bàogào bāokuò nǎxiē nèiróng?
赵　红：马莉，你们的市场调研与分析报告包括哪些内容？

Mǎ Lì：Bàogào zhǔyào bāokuò liù gè bùfen：xùyán、zhǔyào jiélùn、qiánzài de xiāofèi xūqiú、zhǔtǐ nèiróng、wèilái de shìchǎng jīhuì、zuò dà shìchǎng de yíngxiāo jiànyì.
马　莉：报告主要包括六个部分：**序言**、主要结论、**潜在**的消费需求、**主体**内容、未来的市场机会、做大市场的营销建议。

Qí Yuǎn: Diàoyán wènjuàn shèjì dé zěnmeyàng?
齐　远：调研**问卷**设计得怎么样？

Mǎ Lì：Shèjì dé hěn zhuānyè. Duì bèifǎngzhě de xìngbié、niánlíng hé shōurù děng xìnxī zuò le kēxué de pèi’é.
马　莉：设计得很专业。对**被访者**的性别、年龄和收入等信息做了科学的**配额**。

Bǐ’ěr: Cǎiyòng de shì shénme diàoyán fāngshì?
比　尔：采用的是什么调研方式？

Mǎ Lì：Cǎiyòng de shì guójì tōngxíng de CLT，jiùshì jízhōng dìngdiǎn shìchǎng diàoyán fāngshì.
马　莉：采用的是国际**通行**的CLT（Central Location Test），就是集中**定点**市场调研方式。

Zhào Hóng: Dōu zuò le nǎxiē fēnxī?
赵　红：都做了哪些分析？

Mǎ Lì：Yǒu fúzhuāng hángyè jìngzhēng géjú fēnxī、shìchǎng jìngzhēng xiànzhuàng fēnxī、qǐyè shìchǎng zhànyǒulǜ fēnxī、shìchǎng gōngjǐ xiànzhuàng fēnxī . . .
马　莉：有服装行业竞争**格局**分析、市场竞争**现状**分析、企业市场**占有率**分析、市场**供给**现状分析……

Qí Yuǎn: Tāmen de wènjuàn diàochá de zhǔnquèdù zěnmeyàng?
齐　远：他们的问卷调查的**准确度**怎么样？

Mǎ Lì：Shídì wènjuàn yàngběn zài 500 gè yǐshàng，diàochá zhìxìndù dádào 96% yǐshàng. Diàoyán shùjù néng fǎnyìng mùqián fúzhuānglèi chǎnpǐn zuìxīn de shìchǎng zhuàngkuàng hé xiāofèizhě de qiánzài xiāofèi xūqiú.

马　莉：实地问卷**样本**在500个以上，调查**置信度**达到96%以上。调研**数据**能**反映**目前服装类产品最新的市场**状况**和消费者的潜在消费需求。

Bǐ'ěr: Kànlái tāmen diàoyán de xìjié zuò dé búcuò. Zhǔyào jiélùn shì shénme?
比　尔：看来他们调研的细节做得不错。主要结论是什么？

Mǎ Lì: Yī、pǐnpáihuà chéngwéi fāzhǎn zhǔliú; èr、xiāofèi céngcì zài shēngjí. Zhè liǎngdiǎn duì wǒmen hěn zhòngyào, yīnwéi wǒmen gōngsī de fúwù duìxiàng jiù shì gāoduān kèhùqún.
马　莉：一、品牌化成为发展**主流**；二、消费**层次**在**升级**。这两点对我们很重要，因为我们公司的服务**对象**就是高端客户群。

Qí Yuǎn: Yǐjīng bādiǎn le! Jīntiān jiù liáo dào zhèr ba.
齐　远：已经八点了！今天就聊到这儿吧。

Text 1

So your company is also carrying out market research

Today, Qi Yuan and Zhao Hong come to Mary's to help her learn business Chinese. Bill comes too.

Bill: What will you study today?

Maria: Let's talk about topics concerning market research.

Zhao Hong: OK.

Bill: So your company is also doing market research. I'm busy doing that as well.

Maria: Our products will enter Chinese market. Of course we have to do the market research, as the saying goes "Know ourselves and know our rivals as well".

Bill: Right! Marketing itself means research and investigation.

Maria: Yes, scientific and executable research findings may help enterprises make important decisions.

Qi Yuan: Now there are many specialized market research firms and you can ask them for help.

Maria: Yes, our market research project for consumer demand is open for bids from the general public.

Bill: How is it going?

Maria: At present, an enterprise planning firm has already completed a market research and analysis report for us.

Bill: You can be relaxed by entrusting it to others. And I have to do it myself in my company.

Maria: Of course! You are an expert on this.

Zhao Hong: Mary, what are the contents of your market research and analysis report?

Maria: The report mainly includes six parts: introduction, major findings, potential consumers' demand, body contents, future market opportunities, advice on the promotion of market.

Qi Yuan: How is the design of the questionnaire?

Maria: It is very professionally designed. Such information as gender, age and income of the subjects are scientifically allocated.

Bill: What method of research is adopted?

Maria: We adopted the internationally received CLT, which means Central Location Test.

Zhao Hong: What kinds of analyses are conducted?

Maria:There are analysis of the competitive pattern of the garment industry, analysis of the current situation of market competition, analysis of the market occupation ratio of enterprises, and analysis of the current situation of market supply…

Qi Yuan: What about the accuracy of their questionnaire?

Maria: The number of completed samples is more than 500; the confidence level of the research is over 96%. The research results may reflect the latest market situation of garment products and the potential demands of the consumers.

Bill: It seems they have well taken care of the research details. What are the main findings?

Maria: First, brands have become the mainstream; second, the level of consumption is being upgraded. And those two points are both important to us, because our company target to high-end customers.

Qi Yuan: It's already 8 o'clock! Let's stop here today.

生词 New words

1	知己知彼	zhījǐzhībǐ	know ourselves and know our rivals as well
2	科学	kēxué	scientific
3	结论	jiélùn	conclusion
4	重大	zhòngdà	great; important
5	决策	juécè	make decision
6	专门	zhuānyè	specialized
7	需求	xūqiú	demand
8	眼下	yǎnxià	now; at present
9	企划	qǐhuà	enterprise planning
10	委托	wěituō	entrust
11	轻松	qīngsōng	relaxed
12	专家	zhuānjiā	expert; specialist
13	序言	xùyán	introduction
14	潜在	qiánzài	potential
15	主体	zhǔtǐ	subject; main part
16	问卷	wènjuàn	questionnaire
17	被访者	bèifǎngzhě	respondent
18	配额	pèi'é	quota
19	通行	tōngxíng	well-received
20	定点	dìngdiǎn	a designated location
21	格局	géjú	structure; pattern
22	现状	xiànzhuàng	current situation
23	占有率	zhànyǒulǜ	occupation ratio
24	供给	gōngjǐ	supply
25	准确度	zhǔnquèdù	accuracy
26	样本	yàngběn	specimen; sample
27	置信度	zhìxìndù	the confidence level
28	数据	shùjù	data
29	反映	fǎnyìng	to reflect
30	状况	zhuàngkuàng	situation
31	主流	zhǔliú	mainstream
32	层次	céngcì	level
33	升级	shēngjí	to upgrade
34	对象	duìxiàng	object; target

注释 Notes

1. 我们的产品要进入中国市场，当然少不了要做市场调研，知己知彼嘛。

Our products will enter the Chinese market. Of course we have to do the market research, as the saying goes "Know ourselves and know our rivals as well".

可能补语表示主观或客观条件是否允许某种情况发生。可能补语的基本格式是：

Potential Complement indicates whether the subjective or objective conditions allow an event to take place. The basic pattern of potential complement is as follows:

动词+可能补语Verb (V)+ Potential Complement			
肯定式 Affirmative Form	动词 Verb (v)	得	补语 Complement
否定式 Negative Form		不	

在"得、不"后常是表示结果和趋向意思的词语。例如：

Following "得、不" are usually words denoting result or trend. For example:

肯定式Affirmative Form	**否定式**Negative Form
听得清楚	听不清楚
看得见	看不见
进得来	进不来

"得了(liǎo)"或"不了(liǎo)"也可以用在动词后面作可能补语，表示肯定和否定，表示"能怎么样"或"不能怎么样"。例如：

"得了(liǎo)" 或 "不了(liǎo)" may also be used after the verb as potential complement, indicating affirmative and negative, viz., "may…" or "may not…". For example:

肯定式Affirmative Form	**否定式**Negative Form
走得了	走不了
办得了	办不了
吃得了	吃不了

"少不了"是不能缺少、不能避免的意思，例如：

"少不了" means "can't do without" or "can't avoid". For example:

(1) 来中国，少不了要和中国人打交道。

If you go to China, you can't avoid dealing with the Chinese.

（2）有求于人，少不了要多说几句好话。

If you need help from others, you have to say a few compliments.

（3）要更好地开发新产品，少不了要进行市场调研。

In order to better develop new products, you have to conduct market research.

2. 我们的产品要进入中国市场，当然少不了要做市场调研，知己知彼嘛。

Our products will enter the Chinese market. Of course we have to do the market research, as the saying goes "Know ourselves and know our rivals as well".

《孙子兵法·谋攻》中有："知彼知己，百战不殆"。意思是对敌人和自己的情况都非常了解，打仗的时候才不会输。后来常常用"知己知彼"来说要正确估计自己，也要深刻了解对方，做事情才能成功。有时单用前一句，有时两句连用。

In "Attacking Strategies" of ***The Art of War*** there is a saying "知彼知己，百战不殆", means "Those who know themselves and know their opponents as well will win every battle of a war." Later "知己知彼" is used to indicate that for the success of competition, you have to have right estimation of yourself and know your rival well. Sometimes only the first half of the saying is used, sometimes the complete saying is adopted.

3. 我们的产品要进入中国市场，当然少不了要做市场调研，知己知彼嘛。

Our products will enter the Chinese market, of course we have to the market research, as the saying goes "Know ourselves and know our rivals as well".

"嘛"，语气助词，读轻声，常在口语中放在陈述句末尾，表示事情就是这样或者是道理很明显。句末语调用降调。例如：

"嘛", an exclamatory word with a light tone, usually put at the end of narrative sentence, indicating "this is the way things are" or "it's obvious that…". A falling tone is applied at the end of the sentence. For example:

（1）他本来就是我们的经理嘛。

He is our manager after all.

（2）你有什么话就说嘛。

Just speak up your mind.

（3）他们自己要去的嘛，我也没办法。

They themselves wanted to go and I couldn't do anything about it.

4．眼下，已经有一家北京的企划公司为我们做好了一份市场调研与分析报告。

At present, an enterprise planning firm has already completed a market research and analysis report for us.

“眼下”，名词，意思是目前、现在，例如：

“眼下”, noun, means at present, now. For example:

（1）眼下物价涨得很厉害。

Now the prices are soaring.

（2）眼下公司的资金有点儿短缺。

Now the company is lacking in funds.

（3）眼下一点儿现货都没有了。

At present no stock is available.

5．企业市场占有率分析……

analysis of the market occupation ratio of enterprises...

“占有率”中的“率”指两个相关的数在一定条件下的比值，如增长率、离婚率、税率等。

“率” in “占有率” refers to the ratio between two numbers, such as growth rate, divorce rate, tax rate.

（1）十年来，中国西部地区GDP年均增长率达到了11.42%。

During the last decade, the annual growth rate of GDP for the western region of China reaches 11.42%.

（2）2008年，北京成为全国离婚率最高的城市之一。

In 2008, Beijing became one of the cities with the highest divorce rate.

（3）据说北欧国家对富人征收很高的个人所得税，税率在70%以上。

It is reported that the northern European counties levy a very high income tax on the rich people, with the tax rate exceeding 70%.

课文二

Zánmen jiù cóng zhè jǐ ge fāngmiàn lái diàoyán

咱们就从这几个方面来调研

Bǐ'ěr dàilǐng shìchǎngbù de liǎng wèi fù jīnglǐ hé liǎng míng zhùlǐ zhāokāi yèwù huìyì, tǎolùn rúhé kāizhǎn bǐjìběn diànnǎo de xiāofèizhě xūqiú hé shìchǎng dìngwèi de shìchǎng diàoyán.

比尔带领市场部的两位副经理和两名助理召开业务会议，讨论如何开展笔记本电脑的消费者需求和市场定位的市场调研。

Bǐ'ěr：Dàjiā hǎo！Gōngsī yào kāifā xīn chǎnpǐn，yāoqiú wǒmen shìchǎngbù kāizhǎn yí cì shìchǎng diàoyán,yǐbiàn zuò chū zhèngquè de xīn chǎnpǐn dìngwèi. Zánmen tǎolùn yíxià shìchǎng diàoyán de nèiróng.

比　尔：大家好！公司要开发新产品，要求我们**市场部**开展一次市场调研，**以便**作出正确的新产品**定位**。咱们讨论一下市场调研的内容。

Lǐ fù jīnglǐ：Shǒuxiān yào zuò xīn chǎnpǐn de kěxíngxìng yánjiū，kěyǐ cóng xiàmian jǐ ge fāngmiàn rùshǒu：shìchǎng róngliàng、jìngzhēng duìshǒu、jìngzhēng chéngdù、qiánzài de xūqiú.

李副经理：首先要做新产品的**可行性**研究，可以从下面几个方面入手：市场**容量**、竞争**对手**、竞争**程度**、潜在的需求。

Liú fù jīnglǐ：Duì chǎnpǐn gàiniàn jiēshòudù de cèshì yě shì yǒu bìyào de. Zhèyàng wǒmen jiù néng liǎojiě dào：shìchǎng xūqiúliàng、héxīn xiāofèiqún、qiánzài xiāofèiqún hé fāzhǎnxìng xiāofèiqún.

刘副经理：对产品**概念**接受度的测试也是有**必要**的。这样我们就能了解到：市场**需求量**、**核心消费群**、**潜在消费群**和**发展性消费群**。

Zhùlǐ xiǎo Zhōu：Zánmen de diàoyán fànwéi kěyǐ xuǎndìng Běijīng，duì xiāofèi qúntǐ zuò xìfēn hé dìngwèi.

助理小周：咱们的调研**范围**可以**选定**北京，对**消费群体**作**细分**和定位。

Bǐ'ěr：Yào liǎojiě bùtóng tèzhēng rénqún de xūqiú,kànkan shuí huì shì zánmen de qiánzài kèhù. Kěyǐ gēnjù yìxiē tèzhēng lái xìfēn xiāofèi qúntǐ.

比　尔：要了解不同特征**人群**的需求，看看谁会是咱们的潜在客户。可以根据一些特征来细分消费群体。

Zhùlǐ xiǎo Qián：Xìfēn de tèzhēng yìbān bāokuō niánlíng、xìngbié、shēnghuó xíguàn、shēnghuó shuǐpíng、jiàzhíguān děng.

助理小钱：细分的特征一般包括年龄、性别、生活习惯、生活水平、**价值观**等。

Bǐ'ěr：Kěyǐ.

比　尔：可以。

Lǐ fù jīnglǐ：Guānyú yònghù xūqiú yánjiū,wǒ liè le liù gè fāngmiàn：(yī) pǐnpái qīngxiàng，(èr) chǎnpǐn gōngnéng，(sān) jiàgé qīwàng，(sì) cùxiāo tuīguǎng，(wǔ) gòumǎi qúdào，liù fúwù tǐyàn.

李副经理：关于**用户**需求研究，我列了六个方面：(一)品牌倾向，(二)产品**功能**，(三)价格**期望**，(四)促销推广，(五)购买渠道，(六)服务**体验**。

Bǐ'ěr: Hěn quánmiàn. Wǒ kàn zánmen jiù cóng zhè jǐ gè fāngmiànlái diàoyán.
比　尔：很全面。我看咱们就从这几个方面来调研。

Liú fù jīnglǐ: Bié wàng le hái yīnggāi yánjiū yánjiū zánmen de jìngzhēngzhě. Zhè dāngzhōng yào liǎojiě Lenovo、Acer、HP děng zhòngdiǎn chǎngshāng yǐ yǒu de shìchǎng guīmó、jìngzhēng cèlüè hé shìchǎng fèn'é.
刘副经理：别忘了还应该研究研究咱们的**竞争者**。这当中要了解Lenovo、Acer、HP等**重点厂商**已有的市场**规模**、竞争策略和市场**份额**。

Lǐ fù jīnglǐ: Háiyào zhùyì qiánzài de jìngzhēngzhě hé tìdài chǎnpǐn de fēnxī.
李副经理：还要注意潜在的竞争者和**替代**产品的分析。

Bǐ'ěr: Duì, zhījǐzhībǐ, bǎizhànbúdài ma!
比　尔：对，知己知彼，百战不殆嘛！

Liú fù jīnglǐ: Nà wǒmen jiù gēnjù zhèxiē qíngkuàng lái shèjì diàochá wènjuàn.
刘副经理：那我们就根据这些情况来设计调查问卷。

Bǐ'ěr: Hǎo! Shèjì wènjuàn shí, yào bǎ dìngxìng de wèntí hé dìngliàng wèntí jiéhé qilai. Jì yào wèn "wéishénme", yě yào wèn "yǒu duōshǎo?" "shì shénme ?" "fāshēng le shénme ? " zhèyàng de wèntí.
比　尔：好！设计问卷时，要把**定性**问题和**定量**问题结合起来。既要问"为什么"，也要问"有多少?""是什么?""发生了什么?"这样的问题。

Lǐ fù jīnglǐ: Duì, dìngliàng wèntí de shùliàng yào chōngfèn, zhèyàng cáinéng zuò chū zhǔnquè de tǒngjì fēnxī.
李副经理：对，定量问题的数量要**充分**，这样才能作出准确的**统计**分析。

Bǐ'ěr: Shìchǎng diàoyán de liǎng gè zhǔyào huánjié shì xìnxī shōují hé diàoyán fēnxī. Xìnxī shōují yóu liú fù jīnglǐ fùzé, xià zhōuwǔ zhīqián wánchéng.
比　尔：市场调研的两个主要环节是信息收集和调研分析。信息收集由刘副经理负责，下周五之前完成。

Liú fù jīnglǐ: Méi wèntí.
刘副经理：没问题。

Bǐ'ěr: Diàoyán fēnxī yóu Lǐ fù jīnglǐ fùzé. Lǐ fù jīnglǐ, qǐng nǐ gēnjù diàochá jiéguǒ zuò chū yí fèn bàogào.
比　尔：调研分析由李副经理负责。李副经理，请你根据调查结果做出一份报告。

Lǐ fù jīnglǐ：Hǎo de.
李副经理：好的。

Bǐ' ěr：Dàjiā hái yǒu shénme wèntí ma？Méi wèntí jiù sànhuì.
比　尔：大家还有什么问题吗？没问题就**散会**。

Text 2

Let's do the research in these aspects

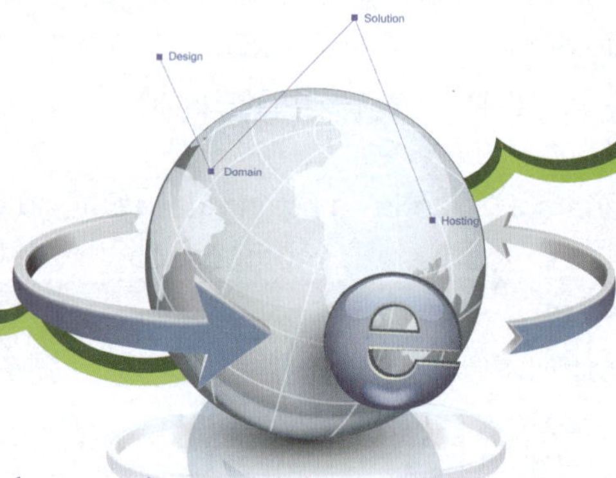

Bill, his two vice managers and two assistants are having a meeting to discuss how to conduct the market research on the consumer demand and market orientation for notebook computers.

Bill: Hi everybody! Our company plans to develop a new product and requires our marketing department to conduct a market research, so as to have a clear definition of the new product's orientation in the market. Now let's discuss the contents of our market research.

Vice Manager Li: First of all we have to conduct a feasibility study of the new product, starting from the following aspects: market capacity, competitive rivals, competitive degree and potential demand.

Vice Manager Liu: A test of the consumer acceptability to the product concept is also necessary. So we can have adequate knowledge about the market capacity, core customer groups, potential customer groups and expanding consumer groups.

Assistant Xiaozhou: Our research might be confined to the area of Beijing for segmentation and definition of the consumer groups.

Bill: We must understand the demands of different groups of people in order to locate our potential customers. And the customer groups might be segmented according to relevant characteristics.

Assistant Xiaoqian: The characteristics used for segmentation are age, gender, living habits, living standards and values.

Bill: Good.

Vice Manager Li: About user demand, I list six aspects: one, brand orientation; two, product functions; three, price expectation; four, sale and promotions; five, purchase channels; six, service experience.

Bill: That's pretty comprehensive. I think we should conduct the research from these six aspects.

Vice Manager Liu: Don't forget to study our competitors, especially the market size, competitive strategies and market share of such major manufacturers as Lenovo, Acer and HP.

Vice Manager Li: And we have to pay attention to the analysis of potential competitors and alternative products.

Bill: Right, Those who know themselves and know their opponents as well will win every battle of a war.

Vice Manager Liu: Then we'll design the questionnaire based on these conditions.

Bill: Good! When we design the questionnaire, we should combine qualitative and quantitative questions. As we ask "why?", we must ask also questions like "how much?" "what is it?" "what happens?"

Vice Manager Li: Agreed, the number of quantitative questions must be sufficient, so we can have an accurate statistical analysis.

Bill: The two major procedures of a market research are information collection and research analysis. Liu will be responsible for the information collection, please finish before next Friday.

Vice Manager Liu: No problem.

Bill: Li will be responsible for research analysis. Li, please submit a report based on the research findings.

Vice Manager Li: OK.

Bill: Do you still have any questions? If not, the meeting is over.

生词 New words

1	市场部	shìchǎngbù	marketing department
2	以便	yǐbiàn	so as to

3	定位	dìngwèi	orientation
4	可行性	kěxíngxìng	feasibility
5	容量	róngliàng	capacity
6	对手	duìshǒu	rival
7	程度	chéngdù	level; degree
8	概念	gàiniàn	idea; concept
9	必要	bìyào	necessary
10	需求量	xūqiúliàng	demand
11	核心消费群	héxīn xiāofèiqún	core customer group
12	潜在消费群	qiánzài xiāofèiqún	potential customer group
13	发展性消费群	fāzhǎnxìng xiāofèiqún	expanding customer group
14	范围	fànwéi	range; scope
15	选定	xuǎndìng	confine
16	消费群体	xiāofèi qúntǐ	consumer group
17	细分	xìfēn	segmentation
18	人群	rénqún	groups of people
19	价值观	jiàzhíguān	value
20	用户	yònghù	user
21	功能	gōngnéng	function
22	期望	qīwàng	expectation; hope
23	体验	tǐyàn	experience
24	竞争者	jìngzhēngzhě	competitor
25	重点	zhòngdiǎn	major
26	厂商	chǎngshāng	manufacture
27	规模	guīmó	size
28	份额	fèn'é	quotient; share
29	替代	tìdài	alternative

30	定性	dìngxìng	qualitative
31	定量	dìngliàng	quantitative
32	充分	chōngfèn	sufficient
33	统计	tǒngjì	statistical
34	散会	sànhuì	the meeting is over

注释 Notes

公司要开发新产品，要求我们市场部开展一次市场调研，以便作出正确的新产品定位。

Our company plans to develop a new product and requires our marketing department to conduct a market research, so as to have a clear definition of the new product's orientation in the market.

“以便”是连词，用在目的复句中。常常连接两个分句，用在后一个分句的开头，表示前一个分句所说的条件，使得后一个分句所说的目的容易实现。例如：

“以便” is a conjunction, used in a composite sentence denoting a purpose. It usually combines two clauses, used at the beginning of the second clause, indicating the condition of the first clause makes it easier to realize the purpose of the second clause.

（1）你让他住在我家吧，以便我更好地照顾他。
Just let him stay in my home, so I can better take care of him.

（2）我留了张条子以便和她联系。
I kept a note for future contact with her.

（3）我决定学习汉语以便在北京更好地生活。
I decided to learn Chinese to make my life here in Beijing even better.

附录

市场调查问卷样例

2009年北京市笔记本电脑消费者需求市场调研

性别：

男（ ）；女（ ）。

年龄：

18岁以下（ ）； 18—25岁（ ）；26—30岁（ ）；

31—35岁（ ）；36—40岁（ ）；41岁以上（ ）。

职业：

公司（ ）；机关事业单位（ ）；工商业者（ ）；教育工作者（ ）；

学生（ ）；工人（ ）； 农民（ ）； 司机（ ）；

其他：

月收入：

1000元以下（ ）；1000-2000元（ ）；2001-3000元（ ）；

3001-4000元（ ）；4001-5000元（ ）；5001-6000元（ ）；

6001-7000元（ ）；7001-8000元（ ）；8001元-10000元（ ）；

10000元以上（ ）。

1．您使用过以下哪种品牌的电脑？

- 联想

- 方正
- 同方
- 戴尔
- 苹果
- 索尼
- 其他：

2．您上次购买您的电脑产品是什么时候？

- 一个月以内
- 一个月到六个月
- 六个月到一年
- 不确定
- 其他：

3．您最初是怎样了解到您所购买的电脑产品的？

- 收音机
- 报纸
- 杂志
- 互联网
- 亲戚/朋友/同事
- 不确定

- 其他：

4．您怎样评价您所购买的电脑产品？

- 差
- 一般
- 好
- 很好
- 非常优秀

5．您会把您购买的电脑品牌推荐给朋友或同事吗？

- 一定不会
- 可能不会
- 不确定
- 可能会
- 一定会

6．您今后再次购买同类电脑产品的可能性有多大？

- 非常不可能
- 不怎么可能
- 不确定
- 可能
- 很可能

7．您更愿意接受什么价位的电脑？

- 2000-3000元
- 3000-4000元
- 4000-5000元
- 5000-6000元
- 6000元以上

8．您购买电脑时，优先考虑什么因素？

- 品牌
- 外观
- 体积
- 配置
- 性价比
- 售后服务
- 其他：

9．如果您购买的电脑产品有什么要改进的，您最希望的是什么？

10．您认为最好的国产电脑品牌是哪一个？为什么？

11．您认为最好的国外电脑品牌是哪一个？为什么？

12．您更喜欢国产品牌还是国外品牌？为什么？

13．其他的意见及建议：

练习
Exercises

一、跟读生词并且纠音。
Read the new words after the teacher and correct your pronunciation.

二、跟读课文并且纠音。
Read the text after the teacher and correct your pronunciation.

三、学生分组，分角色朗读课文一、二。
Divide the students into groups and read the texts 1 & 2 in different roles.

四、学生分组，不看书表演课文一、二。
Divide the students into groups and role play the texts 1 & 2 without referring to the book.

五、角色扮演。（提示：角色可以互换。）
Role play (Note:The roles can be exchanged.)

请参考课文一、二，使用课文中的语句完成下面的对话。

1. A是某调研公司的经理，B是客户，两个人谈谈市场调研的问题。
   提示：B提出问题和要求；A回答将怎样根据客户的要求设计和完成市场调研。

2. A、B是某公司市场部的两位副经理，两个人谈谈怎样设计关于某产品消费者市场需求的调查问卷。

六、替换练习。
Substitution drills.

1. <u>产品要进入中国市场，当然少不了要做市场调研，知己知彼</u> + 嘛。
   你看市场调研确实很有必要
   我们可以找专业的市场调研公司帮我们
   我们的市场调研方案也可以向社会公开招标
   你们的调研问卷设计得很专业

2. 眼下，+ 一家企划公司为我们做好了一份市场调研与分析报告。

越来越多的中国产品走向世界

很多外商选择在中国投资办厂

外商独资、中外合资的企业越来越多

很多企业都很重视市场调研工作

3. 企业市场+ 占有 + 率 + 不断提高。

新产品	合格	不断提高
企业职工	失业	逐年降低
大学生	就业	逐年提高
年轻人	结婚	有所减少
中年人	离婚	有所增加
人口年	增长	有所减少

七、把下面的词语组成句子。

Make a sentence with the following words.

课文一：

1. 我们 公司 市场 在 调研 做

2. 我们 产品 市场 中国 的 要 进入

3. 结论 企业 决策 科学 重大 的 能够 帮助 做出

4. 公开 调研 我们 社会 方案 向 就 招标 是 的

5. 你 方面 专家 市场 是 调研 的

6. 设计 调研 怎么样 问卷 得

7. 什么 调研 的 你们 方式 公司 采用 是

8. 的 问卷 怎么样 准确度 他们 调查

9. 细节 他们 看来 调研 做 的 得 不错

10. 的　对象　就　是　高端　我们　客户群　公司　服务

课文二：

1. 市场　公司　我们　一　开展　市场部　次　要求　调研

2. 要　可行性　新　研究　做　产品　首先　的

3. 接受度　必要　测试　有　也　产品　对　的　概念　是

4. 谁　的　客户　咱们　是　潜在　看看　会

5. 来　一些　群体　根据　细分　可以　消费　特征

6. 就　调研　这　看　几　我　从　方面　咱们　个　来

7. 竞争者　了　别　研究　咱们　应该　还　忘　的

8. 来　情况　根据　就　这些　问卷　设计　那　我们　调查

9. 收集　负责　信息　刘　由　经理

10. 你　报告　根据　结果　一　份　做出　请　调查

八、用"……不了"完成下面的句子。

Rewrite the following sentences with "……不了".

1. 你点的菜太多了，我们吃不完。
2. 银行已经关门了，我们今天不能取钱了。
3. 要开发新产品，肯定要做市场调研。
4. 他病了，今天不能来上班了。
5. 老板有事，今天的会议不能开了。
6. 公司晚上开会，我们不能去看球赛了。

九、用“以便”完成下面的句子。

Rewrite the following sentences with “以便”.

1. 为了更好地了解中国文化，他来北京学习汉语。
2. 为了更好地满足未来客户的需求，他们公司准备做市场调研。
3. 为了作出准确的统计分析，定量问题的数量一定要充分。
4. 为了提高问卷调查的准确度，实地问卷样本要在500个以上。
5. 去面试时，着装要整洁，要给面试官留下好印象。

十、完成对话。

Complete the dialogue.

1. A：你最近忙什么呢？
   B：______________________________。
2. A：你们的市场调研与分析报告包括哪些方面？
   B：______________________________。
3. A：你们的调查问卷设计得怎么样？
   B：______________________________。
4. A：你们采用的是什么调研方式？
   B：______________________________。
5. A：你们的市场调研都做了哪些分析？
   B：______________________________。
6. A：你们的问卷调查的准确度怎么样？
   B：______________________________。
7. A：你们的市场调研的主要结论是什么？
   B：______________________________。
8. A：如果要做新产品的可行性研究，可以从哪些方面入手？
   B：______________________________。

9. A：你们的调研范围选定在哪儿？
   B：______________________________。

10. A：你们根据什么特征来细分消费群体？
    B：______________________________。

十一、阅读理解。

Reading comprehension.

比尔最近一直在忙市场调研的事情。现在有很多专业的调研公司，可是比尔认为市场调研要有针对性，所以他的电脑公司想自己做市场调研。

首先，在电脑产品方面，他们公司想了解国内的电脑市场有什么新产品和新技术，这样才能更好地开发自己公司的产品。

其次，他们公司也要了解国内电脑产品的价格情况。因为很多商家都在打“价格战”，产品的价格也是吸引顾客的重要方面之一。

最后，他们公司希望通过市场调研，帮助他们找到理想的电脑零部件供应商。他们想根据调研报告，比较一下几家大的供应商，哪家的价格比较便宜，哪家的信用比较好，还有哪家的供货速度比较快。

虽然市场调研费时费力，可是它直接关系着公司未来的发展，可以说是至关重要。所以比尔公司的上上下下都非常重视这次市场调研。

回答问题。Answer the questions.

1. 比尔最近在忙什么呢？

2. 比尔的公司打算自己做市场调研还是请调研公司帮他们做？

3. 比尔的公司打算怎么做市场调研？

4. 比尔公司的市场调研包括哪几个方面？

5. 为什么市场调研很重要？

十二、复述课文一和课文二。

Retell the texts 1 & 2.

十三、完成任务。

Complete the following tasks.

1．请问你工作过的公司做过市场调研吗？如果做过，请介绍这家公司做市场调研的具体情况，比如说怎么做市场调研？涉及哪些方面？有什么重要环节？具体做了哪些方面的分析？如果没做过，请向你的同学或是朋友询问相关的情况。

2．小组活动：2-4个人一组，自己选定题目，比如调查中国老百姓外出就餐的情况、大学生日常上网的情况、学校周边的餐饮娱乐设施情况等等。

活动任务：

（1）设计一份调查问卷，去街边作问卷调查，至少要收回10份问卷，请根据调查结果，写出书面调查报告。

（2）请把你们的调查问卷和调查报告带到课堂上来，向你的老师和同学介绍。

（3）请每组的成员在课堂上介绍你们在街上作问卷调查的情况。

设计调查问卷时请注意下面的问题：

（1）要根据以下特征来细分调查群体，如年龄、性别、生活习惯、生活水平等。

（2）要设计包含以下内容的问题，如为什么、有多少、是什么、发生了什么等。

Unit 6

第六单元

Shāngwù yíngxiāo

商务营销

Business Marketing

课文一

Hěn duō pǐnpái de diànnǎo dōu zài jiàngjià cùxiāo

很多品牌的电脑都在降价促销

Zhào Hóng yào xiě yífèn yíngxiāo fāng'àn, kěshì tājiā lǐ de diànnǎo huài le. Qí Yuǎn péi tā zài Zhōngguāncūn de Hǎilóng Dàshà lǐ mǎi diànnǎo.

赵红要写一份营销方案，可是她家里的电脑坏了。齐远陪她在中关村的海龙大厦里买电脑。

Zhào Hóng: Jīntiān shāngchǎng lǐ de rén zěnme zhème duō?
赵　红：今天商场里的人怎么这么多？

Qí Yuǎn: Zhōumò rén zǒngshì hěn duō. Érqiě, zhè liǎng tiān shì Zhōngguāncūn diànnǎo jié, hěn duō pǐnpái de diànnǎo dōu zà jiàngjià cùxiāo.
齐　远：周末人总是很多。而且，这两天是中关村电脑节，很多品牌的电脑都在降价促销。

Zhào Hóng: Guàibude qián liǎng tiān wǒ yǒu hǎo jǐ gè tóngxué dōu mǎi le diànnǎo.
赵　红：怪不得前两天我有好几个同学都买了电脑。

Qí Yuǎn: Kàn nàge guǎnggào——dǎzhé jiā mǎi yī sòng yī jiā chōujiǎng, guòqù kànkan!
齐　远：看那个广告——**打折**+买一送一+**抽奖**，过去看看！

Zhào Hóng: Zhè tái bǐjìběn diànnǎo duōshǎo qián?
赵　红：这台**笔记本电脑**多少钱？

Xiāoshòuyuán: Bā qiān bā bǎi liù shí bā yuán. Xiànzài wǒmen zài gǎo yōuhuì huódòng, nín rúguǒ xiànzài mǎi, kěyǐ dǎ jiǔ zhé, hái huì sòng nín yí gè liù shí G de yídòng yìngpán, nín hái kěyǐ cānjiā wǒmen dàshà de chōujiǎng huódòng, zhòngjiǎnglǜ bǎi fēn zhī bǎi, yīděngjiǎng shì XīnMǎTài shuāngrén yóu.
销售员：8868元。现在我们在**搞**优惠活动，您如果现在买，可以打九折，还会送您一个60G的**移动硬盘**，您还可以参加我们**大厦**的抽奖活动，**中奖率**100%，**一等奖**是**新马泰**双人游。

Qí Yuǎn: Quèshí bǐ píngshí yōuhuì bùshǎo.
齐　远：确实比平时优惠不少。

Zhào Hóng: Bù zhīdào nǐmen de shòuhòu fúwù zěnmeyàng?
赵　红：不知道你们的售后服务怎么样？

Xiāoshòuyuán: Yìbān bǐjìběn diànnǎo de bǎoxiūqī shì yìnián, wǒmen de bǎoxiūqī shì sānnián.
销售员：一般笔记本电脑的**保修期**是一年，我们的保修期是三年。

Qí Yuǎn: Fúwù búcuò a! Kànlái diànnǎo hángyè de jìngzhēng yuè lái yuè jīliè le.
齐　远：服务不错啊！看来电脑行业的竞争越来越激烈了。

Zhào Hóng: Qián jǐ tiān wǒ zài diànshì shàng kàn dào yí gè guǎnggào ——sì qiān bā bǎi bā, diànnǎo bān huí jiā! Yàobù wǒmen xiān qù kànkan zhègè páizi de diànnǎo?
赵　红：前几天我在电视上看到一个广告——四千八百八，电脑**搬**回家！要不我们先去看看这个**牌子**的电脑？

Qí Yuǎn: Hǎo a.
齐　远：好啊。

（Tāmen lái dào le lìng yí gè guìtái qián.）
（他们来到了另一个柜台前。）
Zhào Hóng: Zhè jiù shì diànshì guǎnggào shàng shuō de nà kuǎn diànnǎo ma?
赵　红：这就是电视广告上说的那款电脑吗？

Xiāoshòuyuán: Duì, rúguǒ nín xiànzài mǎi zhè kuǎn diànnǎo, yǒu lǐwù zèngsòng, hái kěyǐ cānjiā wǒmen de chōujiǎng huódòng.
销售员：对，如果您现在买这**款**电脑，有礼物**赠送**，还可以参加我们的抽奖活动。

Qí Yuǎn: Guǎnggào zuò dé tǐng jīngcǎi de, kě pèizhì bù zěnmeyàng. Wǒmen zài kànkan biéde páizi ba.
齐　远：广告做得挺**精彩**的，可**配置**不怎么样。我们再看看别的牌子吧。

Text 1

Many brand computers are on sale

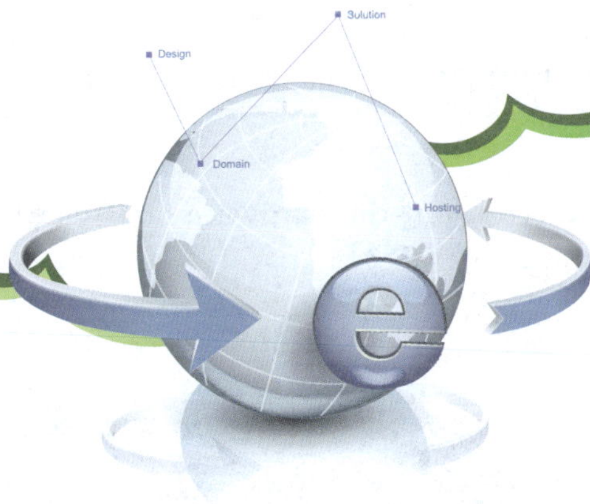

Zhao Hong needs to write a marketing plan, but her computer at home has broken down. Qi Yuan accompanies her to buy a computer in Hailong Tower of Zhongguancun.

Zhao Hong: Why are there so many people in the shops?

Qi Yuan: There are always a lot of people during weekends. And besides, Zhongguancun Computer Fair is taking place these days. Many brand computers are on sale.

Zhao Hong: No wonder several of my classmates bought computers a few days ago.

Qi Yuan: Look at that ad—discount + buy one and get one + lucky draw. Let's take a look!

Zhao Hong: How much is this notebook computer?

Salesperson: 8868 Yuan. Now we have special offers. If you buy it now, you can have 10 percent discount and a 60G portable harddisk. You may participate in our lucky draw as well, the winning rate is 100%, the first prize being a trip for two to Singapore, Malaysia and Thailand.

Qi Yuan: It's really much cheaper than usual.

Zhao Hong: What about your after sale services?

Salesperson: Usually a notebook computer has a one-year warranty period, and our warranty period is three years.

Qi Yuan: So great! It seems the competition of the computer industry is getting more and more fierce.

Zhao Hong: A few days ago I saw a TV commercial—Only 4880 Yuan for a computer! Or shall we take a look at this brand?

Qi Yuan: OK.

(They come to another counter.)

Zhao Hong: Is this the computer in the TV commercial?

Salesperson: Yes. If you buy this model, we have gifts for you, and you can participate in our lucky draw.

Qi Yuan: The TV commercial was wonderful, but the hardware configuration is not quite satisfactory. Let's go and look at some other brands.

生词 New words

1	打折	dǎ zhé	to give a discount
2	送	sòng	to give as a present
3	抽奖	chōu jiǎng	lucky draw
4	笔记本电脑	bǐjìběn diànnǎo	notebook computer
5	搞	gǎo	to do; to carry on; to get
6	移动硬盘	yídòng yìngpán	portable harddisk
7	大厦	dàshà	large building; mansion
8	中奖率	zhòngjiǎng lǜ	winning rate
9	一等奖	yīděngjiǎng	first prize
10	保修期	bǎoxiū qī	warranty period
11	搬	bān	to move
12	牌子	páizi	brand; trademark
13	款	kuǎn	a measure word
14	精彩	jīngcǎi	brilliant; splendid; wonderful
15	配置	pèizhì	configuration

专有名词 Proper nouns

1. 中关村
   ZhōngGuānCūn
   Zhongguancun，an avenue which is located in Haidian District of Beijing
2. 海龙大厦
   HǎiLóng DàShà
   Hailong Tower, Electronics Tower
3. 新马泰
   Xīn Mǎ Tài
   abbreviation of Singapore, Malaysia and Thailand

注释 Notes

1. 您如果现在买，可以打九折。

If you buy it now, you can have 10 percent discount.

"打折"是个离合词，两个字中间可以加上1到9的数字。例如：

"打折" is a split word, numbers from 1 to 9 can be put in between the two characters. For example:

（1）100元，打八折，就是80元。
100 Yuan, 20% discount, equals to 80 Yuan.

（2）100元，打一折，就是10元。
100 Yuan, 90% discount, equals to 10 Yuan.

2. 看来电脑行业的竞争越来越激烈了。

It seems the competition of the computer industry is getting more and more fierce.

"看来"表示根据客观情况估计推断。例如：

"看来" indicating a deduction or estimation based on objective conditions. For example:

（1）这个月我们的销售量增加了10%，看来我们的营销方案很有效。

Our sales volume this month has increased by 10%;it seems that our marketing plan is very effective.

（2）便宜的电脑配置都不太高，看来还是一分钱一分货啊！

Cheap computers all have lower hardware configurations; it seems true that one cent of price is one cent of value.

(3)这家公司的信誉不太好，看来我们得换家合作公司了。

The credibility of this company is fishy, it seems we have to find anther company for cooperation.

3. 要不我们先去看看这个牌子的电脑？

Or shall we take a look at the computers of this brand?

"要不"表示"如果不这样"，引出说话人的建议，语气比较委婉。也可以用"要不然"。例如：

"要不" indicates "if not so", introducing the advice of the speaker. The tone is rather soft. "要不然" may also be used. For example:

（1）A：去哪儿呢？故宫已经去过了，长城又太远。

Where shall we go? We have been to the Palace Museum, and the Great Wall is too far from here.

B：要不我们去颐和园吧，那里很漂亮。

Or shall we go to the Summer Palace? It's beautiful there.

（2）A：坐飞机去青岛倒是挺快的，可机票有点儿贵。

To go to Qingdao by plane is fast, but the ticket is a bit expensive.

B：要不然我们坐动车去吧，又快又便宜。

Or let's go there by express train. It's fast and cheap.

4. 广告做得挺精彩的，可配置不怎么样。

The TV commercial was excellent, but the hardware configuration is not quite satisfactory.

“怎么样”代替某种不说出来的动作或情况，这种用法只用于否定式，比直说委婉。“不怎么样”在这里的意思就是“(配置)不好”，但是语气更委婉。例如：

“怎么样” represents an action or condition not expressed explicitly. It can only be used in a negative form and is more tactful than a direct expression. “不怎么样” here simply means “(configuration) not good”, but the tone is more tactful.

（1）那个牌子的电脑并不怎么样，可价格挺高的。

The computer of that brand is not good, but the price is rather high.

（2）他这个人的人品不怎么样。

His moral standing is rather doubtable.

（3）简历上说他的营销经验挺丰富的，可他的营销方案却不怎么样。

He said in his resume he had rich marketing experiences, but his marketing plan is quite fishy.

课文二

Wǒ yào wèi yìkuǎn xīn chē xiě yíngxiāo fāng'àn

我要为一款新车写营销方案

Qí Yuǎn、Zhào Hóng、Bǐ'ěr hé Mǎ Lì zài jiǔba lǐ biān hē biān liáo.

齐远、赵红、比尔和马莉在酒吧里边喝边聊。

Mǎ Lì: Zhào Hóng, hǎo cháng shíjiān dōu méi jiàn dào nǐ le, máng shénme ne?

马　莉：赵红，好长时间都没见到你了，忙什么呢？

Zhào Hóng: Wǒ yào wèi yì kuǎn xīn chē xiě yíngxiāo fāng'àn, wǒmen zhǔguǎn xià zhōu jiù yào, wǒ zhèng zháojí ne. Zhènghǎo jīntiān jiàn dào nǐmen, gǎnkuài bāng wǒ chūchu zhǔyi ba.

赵　红：我要为一款新车写营销方案，我们主管下周就要，我正着急呢。正好今天见到你们，赶快帮我出出主意吧。

Bǐ'ěr: Wǒ juéde zài Zhōngguó zuò guǎnggào zuì yǒuxiào, wǒ jiànyì nǐmen zài bàozhǐ、diànshì, zázhì hé wǎngluò shàng dàliàng de tóufàng guǎnggào.

比　尔：我觉得在中国做广告最有效，我建议你们在报纸、电视、杂志和网络上大量地**投放**广告。

Mǎ Lì: CCTV huángjīn shíduàn de shōushìlǜ hěn gāo, zài nàge shíduàn zuò guǎnggào dehuà, xiàoguǒ yídìng búcuò, hái kěyǐ tígāo nǐmen gōngsī de zhīmíngdù.

马　莉：CCTV**黄金时段**的**收视率**很高，在那个时段做广告的话，效果一定不错，还可以提高你们公司的知名度。

Bǐ'ěr: Hái kěyǐ qǐng míngrén dàiyán a.

比　尔：还可以请**名人代言**啊。

Qí Yuǎn: Búguò xiànzài shàngshì de xīn chē hěn duō, yào xiǎng ràng nǐmen de xīn chē xīyǐn xiāofèizhě, jiù bìxū xiān ràng xiāofèizhě liǎojiě nǐmen de chǎnpǐn de chāyìhuà chéngdù, yě jiù shì liǎojiě nǐmen chǎnpǐn de dútè zhī chù.
齐　远：不过现在**上市**的新车很多，要想让你们的新车吸引消费者，就必须先让消费者了解你们的产品的**差异化**程度，也就是了解产品的**独特**之处。

Zhào Hóng: Méi cuò, chāyìhuà chéngdù shì chǎnpǐn jìngzhēnglì de tǐxiàn. Guǎnggào yídìng yào tūchū wǒmen de qìchē yǔzhòngbùtóng de dìfāng.
赵　红：没错，差异化程度是产品竞争力的体现。广告一定要突出我们的汽车**与众不同**的地方。

Qí Yuǎn: Kāi yí gè xīn chē shàngshì fābùhuì, qǐng yìxiē méitǐ de jìzhě cānjiā. Jìzhě huì zài diànshì、bàozhǐ děng méitǐ shàng bàodào zhè jiàn shì.
齐　远：开一个新车上市**发布会**，请一些媒体的记者参加。记者会在电视、报纸等媒体上**报道**这件事。

Mǎ Lì: Fābùhuì shàng, hái kěyǐ yāoqǐng yì liǎng wèi míngrén shìjià, gǎnshòu xīn chē de shūshìxìng, xiàn shēn shuō fǎ. Tóngshí, yǒu zhuānyè de gōngchéngshī zài xiànchǎng jièshào chē de xìngnéng.
马　莉：发布会上，还可以**邀请**一两位名人**试驾**，**感受**新车的**舒适性**，**现身说法**。同时，有专业的**工程师**在现场介绍车的**性能**。

Qí Yuǎn: Nǐmen hái kěyǐ jiànlì yí gè xīn chē shìjià de lùntán, zài wǎngshàng jìnxíng chǎozuò.
齐　远：你们还可以建立一个新车试驾的**论坛**，在网上进行**炒作**。

Bǐ'ěr: Yě kěyǐ lìyòng ruǎnwén a, qǐng qìchē jùlèbù de chéngyuán zài yìxiē shíshàng bàokān zázhì shàng xiě wénzhāng, yǐndǎo xiāofèi zhě de gòumǎi qīngxiàng.
比　尔：也可以利用**软文**啊，请汽车**俱乐部**的**成员**在一些时尚报刊杂志上写文章，**引导**消费者的购买倾向。

Mǎ Lì: Kěyǐ jiéhé Zhōngguó de jiérì, kāizhǎn "jiérì mǎi chē sòng jīngxǐ "de cùxiāo huódòng.
马　莉：可以**结合**中国的节日，开展“节日买车送**惊喜**”的促销活动。

Zhào Hóng: Háiyǒu, fán zài huódòng qījiān gòumǎi xīn chē de gùkè, dōu néng dédào yí fèn dà lǐbāo.
赵　红：还有，**凡**在活动**期间**购买新车的顾客，都能得到一份大**礼包**。

Bǐ'ěr: Dào qìchē zhǎntīng cānguān de gùkè yě néng huòdé yí fèn jīngměi lǐpǐn, zhèyàng kěyǐ xīyǐn gèng duō de rén lái cānguān nǐmen de xīn chē.
比　尔：到汽车**展厅**参观的顾客也能获得一份**精美**礼品，这样可以吸引更多的人来参观你们的新车。

Qí Yuǎn: Yě kěyǐ qǐng diànshìtái wèi nǐmen gōngsī de lǎobǎn zuò yí gè zhuānfǎng.
齐 远：也可以请电视台为你们公司的老板做一个**专访**。

Mǎ Lì: Duì, tōngguò fǎngwèn bǎ nǐmen qìchē de shèjì lǐniàn、jiàwèi hé xìngnéng děng jièshào gěi xiāofèizhě.
马 莉：对，通过访问把你们汽车的设计理念、**价位**和性能等介绍给消费者。

Zhào Hóng: Nǐmen de diǎnzi tài bàng le! Tài shòu qǐfā le! Duō xiè! Duō xiè! Gǎitiān wǒ qǐng nǐmen chīfàn.
赵 红：你们的**点子**太棒了！太受**启发**了！多谢！多谢！改天我请你们吃饭。

Text 2

I'll write a marketing plan for a new type of car

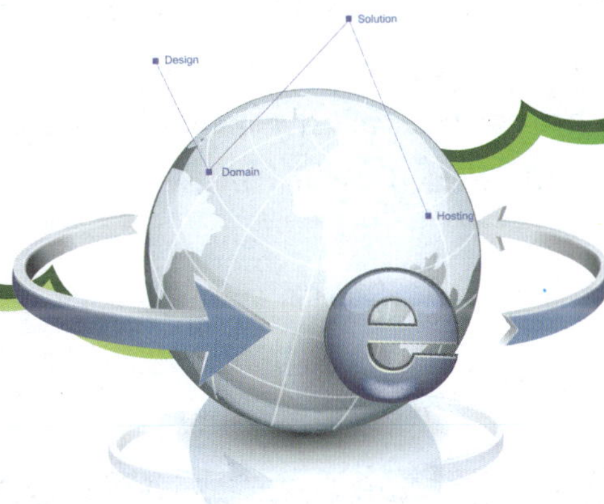

Qi Yuan, Zhao Hong, Bill and Maria are drinking and chatting in a café.

Maria: Zhao Hong, long time no see. What have you been doing?

Zhao Hong: I'm writing a marketing plan for a new type of car. My director wants it next week, I'm really anxious now. Now we're here together, just give me some ideas please.

Bill: I think advertising is the most effective here in China. I advise you to put a lot of ads in media such as newpaper, TV, magazine and Internet.

Maria: The prime time programmes of CCTV have very high ratings. If you put ads in those time slots, the effects will be great, and your company will become more well-known.

Bill: Oh, you may also invite celebrities to be the advertising spokesperson of your product.

Qi Yuan: But there are many new cars on the market. If you want your new car to attract consumers, you must first of all let them know the degree of differentiation of your products or the uniqueness of your product.

Zhao Hong: Yes, the degree of product differentiation represents the competitiveness of the product. The advertisement must highlight the unique characteristics of our car.

Qi Yuan: Just give a press conference and invite journalists from some media. The journalists will report on this in newspapers or on television.

Maria: At the press conference, you can invite one or two celebrities to test-drive the new car and to feel its comfortability by hands-on experiences. In the meanwhile, engineering professionals may introduce the new car's functionalities.

Qi Yuan: You might as well set up a forum for test driving new cars, getting it hyped up on the Internet.

Bill: You may also use soft advertisements by inviting members of auto clubs to write articles in trendy newspapers and magazines, guiding the shopping tendencies of consumers.

Maria: You can hold promotions entitled "Holiday Surprises and Special Offers", combining the

Chinese festivals.

Zhao Hong: And, anyone buying this car during the promotions may get a big gift package.

Bill: The customers visiting the exhibition hall may also get an exquisite gift, and that strategy might attract more people to visit your new car.

Qi Yuan: You may also ask a television station to have an exclusive interview with your boss.

Maria: Yes, through the interview you can introduce the designing concept, price and performance of your new car to the the consumers.

Zhao Hong: Your ideas are great! Very inspiring! Thank you! Thank you so much! I'll invite you to dinner next time.

生词 New words

1	投放	tóufàng	to put
2	黄金时段	huángjīn shíduàn	prime time
3	收视率	shōushì lǜ	audience rating
4	名人	míngrén	the famous person; celebrity
5	代言	dàiyán	to represent
6	上市	shàngshì	to enter the market
7	差异化	chāyìhuà	differentiation
8	独特	dútè	unique
9	与众不同	yǔzhòngbùtóng	be out of the common (or extraordinary)
10	发布会	fābùhuì	press conference
11	报道	bàodào	to report
12	邀请	yāoqǐng	to invite
13	试驾	shìjià	test-drive
14	感受	gǎnshòu	feeling
15	舒适性	shūshìxìng	comfortability
16	现身说法	xiànshēnshuōfǎ	hands-on experiences
17	工程师	gōngchéngshī	engineer

18	性能	xìngnéng	functionality
19	论坛	lùntán	forum
20	炒作	chǎozuò	hype
21	软文	ruǎnwén	advertorial; soft advertisement
22	俱乐部	jùlèbù	club
23	成员	chéngyuán	mumber
24	引导	yǐndǎo	to guide; to lead; to conduct
25	结合	jiéhé	combine; integrate
26	惊喜	jīngxǐ	pleasant surprise
27	凡	fán	every; all
28	期间	qījiān	period of time
29	礼包	lǐbāo	gift package
30	展厅	zhǎntīng	exhibition hall
31	精美	jīngměi	exquisite; elegant
32	专访	zhuānfǎng	exclusive interview
33	价位	jiàwèi	price
34	启发	qǐfā	to inspire
35	点子	diǎnzi	idea

注释 Notes

1. 赶快帮我出出主意吧。

Just give me some ideas please.

“出出主意”，“动词+宾语(V＋O)”结构重叠式是“VV＋O”，宾语不需要重叠。表示动作比较短暂、轻松。例如：

“出出主意”, the repetitive form of the “V+O” pattern is “VV+O” ; the object doesn’t need to be repeaped. It indicates a certain action is rather short and light-hearted. For example:

周末我在家看看书、听听音乐、写写汉字、洗洗衣服，跟朋友一起散散步、逛逛街、聊聊天。

At weekeeds I usually read a bit, listen to some music, write some Chinese charaters, or wash some clothes; maybe I'll take a walk with my friends, go window-shopping or chat together.

2. 要想让你们的新车吸引消费者，就必须先让消费者了解你们产品的差异化程度，也就是了解你们产品的独特之处。

If you want your new car to attract the consumers, you must first of all let them know the uniqueness of your product.

“要”，连词，表示假设，常用于口语中。“要……就……”相当于“要是……就……”，是一个表示假设关系的复句。例如：

“要”, a conjunction, meaning a supposition, usually used in oral language. “要……就……” is similar to “要是……就……”, which is a composite sentence indicating a supposition. For example:

（1）你要不想去那个公司工作，就不要参加他们的面试。

If you don't want to work in that company, don't participate in their interview.

（2）上课的时候，你要不明白，就问一下老师。

At classes, if you don't understand, just ask the teacher.

（3）你要有什么事，就随时给我打电话。

If you need anything, just call me at any time.

3. 凡在活动期间购买新车的顾客，都能得到一份大礼包。

Anyone buying this car during the promotions may get a big gift package.

“凡”，副词，凡是，表示在一定范围里没有例外，有“只要是”的意思。常用在句子的开头。句中常用“都、没有不、就”。例如：

“凡”, adverb; “凡是” indicates no exception to a certain extent and is similar to “只要是”. It is often used at the beginning of a sentence, in which “都、没有不、就” are often used. For example:

（1）凡在经济开发区投资的外商，都能享受政府的优惠政策。

All foreign enterprises that have investments in the economic zone are entitled to the favorable policies of the government.

（2）凡在本商场购买的产品，只要产品完好无损、票据齐全，七日之内均可拿来退还。

All commodities bought in this shop can be refuned within 7 days, as long as they are intact with complete receipts.

（3）凡在本超市消费满100元的顾客都能参加抽奖。

Any customer who spends more than 100 Yuan may participate in the lucky draw.

4．也可以利用软文啊，请汽车俱乐部的成员在一些时尚报刊杂志上写文章，……

You may also use soft advertisements by inviting members of auto clubs to write articles in trendy newspapers and magazines,

“软文”是由企业的市场策划人员或广告公司的文案人员，以记者或新闻工作者的角度来撰写的“文字广告”，也叫“软(文)广告”，是相对于硬广告或纯广告而言的。硬广告就是传统的,如报纸上登的那些非常直白的广告，是专门放在广告栏中的广告文，是一种显明的、凸现的广告形式。而软广告则通过一种更巧妙的、更迂回的、更隐蔽的方式将广告的内容传达出去，使消费者在不知不觉中把广告所传达的内容接受下来。目前软文已成为企业的一种非常实用的宣传手段，因为它常能取得硬广告达不到的效果。

“软文” are “verbal advertisements” written by marketing personnel of enterprises or copywriters of advertising companies, also called “soft advertisements” in contrast with hard advertisements or pure advertisements. Hard advertisements are those traditional and direct ones put in the advertisement columns of newspapers, which is an obvious kind of advertisements. And soft advertisements adopt a more circuitous and covert method to communicate the message, enabling the consumers to unawares accept the contents of the advertisements. Now the soft advertisement has become an effective way of publicity for enterprises, for it can often accomplish results hard advertisements cannot.

练习 Exercises

一、跟读生词并且纠音。
Read the new words after the teacher and correct your pronunciation.

二、跟读课文并且纠音。
Read the text after the teacher and correct your pronunciation.

三、学生分组，分角色朗读课文一、二。
Divide the students into groups and read the texts 1 & 2 in different roles.

四、学生分组，不看书分角色表演课文一、二。
Divide the students into groups and role play the texts 1 & 2 without referring to the book.

五、角色扮演。
Role play.

1．几个人一组，一起讨论下面(1)和(2)的问题。

2．两人一组，分为角色A和B，谈论下面(3)和(4)的问题。A和B的角色可以互换。

提示的问题：

（1）课文一中提到的促销手段有哪些？你还知道哪些？你认为哪种促销手段比较有效？为什么？

（2）如果你本来没有购物的打算，但是看到广告上说：价格很优惠，又赠送礼物；还可以参加抽奖，奖品很丰富！这时你会不会去买？为什么？

（3）课文中提到的营销策略哪种比较有效？如果你是赵红，你会怎么写你的营销方案？

（4）你怎么看请名人代言的广告？怎样才能让这种广告更有效？

六、替换练习。

Substitution drills.

1．广告做得 ＋ 挺 ＋ 精彩 ＋ 的，可 ＋ 配置 ＋ 不怎么样。

这件衣服	便宜	款式
她的英语	流利	汉语
这家公司的待遇	好	工作气氛
他的业务能力	强	管理能力

2．要想＋让你们的新车吸引消费者，就必须＋ 先让消费者了解你们产品的差异化程度。

提高公司的销售量	有一个好的营销方案
适应市场的需求	不断地开发新产品
提高公司的知名度	大量地投放广告
让你们的产品受欢迎	提高你们的售后服务

3．凡＋在活动期间购买新车的顾客，都 ＋ 能得到一份大礼包。

在本超市消费满100元的顾客	能参加抽奖
在本市开发区投资的外商	能享受优惠政策
到我们展厅参加的顾客	能得到一份精美礼物
是市场部的员工	要参加这次市场调研

4. 把＋你们汽车的设计理念、价位和性能等＋介绍给＋ 消费者。

我的中国朋友	你
你们公司的产品	中国消费者
这部电影	你的朋友

七、把下面的词语组成句子。

Make a sentence with the following words.

课文一：

1. 很多　降价　的　电脑　在　品牌　都　促销
2. 电脑　我　怪不得　好几个　有　同学　买了　都　前两天
3. 优惠　我们　现在　搞　在　活动
4. 如果　您　可以　九　现在　买　打……折
5. 您　活动　我们　可以　参加　抽奖　大厦　的
6. 确实　优惠　比　不少　平时
7. 看来　行业　越来越　电脑　的　了　激烈　竞争

课文二：

1. 主意　我　帮　出　赶快　出　吧

2. 广告 我 你们 建议 媒体 在……上 大量 地 投放

3. 黄金 CCTV 收视率 时段 高 的 很

4. 与众不同 广告 要 一定 汽车 突出 我们 地方 的

5. 会 记者 电视 在 报纸 这件事 媒体 上 等 报道

6. 可以 你们 一个 建立 网上 炒作 论坛 在 进行

7. 汽车 到 参观 展厅 礼品 的 能 顾客 也 精美 获得 一份

8. 电视台 请 为 一个 老板 你们 专访 的 做

八、根据课文填空。

Fill in the blank according to the text.

1. 填出合适的动词。

（　　）优惠活动	（　　）新闻发布会
（　　）抽奖活动	（　　）购买倾向
（　　）促销活动	（　　）知名度
（　　）消费者	（　　）礼物
（　　）主意	（　　）广告

2. 填出合适的形容词。

（　　）的竞争	（　　）的广告
（　　）的礼品	（　　）的杂志

九、选词填空。

Choose the words to fill in the blank.

（一）选择合适的动词填空。

抽奖　打……折　代言　建议　邀请　报道　结合　上市

1. 你如果买得多，我可以给你（　　）八（　　）。
2. 只要您在本商场的消费满200元，就可以参加我们的（　　）活动，中将率100%。
3. 买数码产品时，我（　　）你先在网上查好价格，再去中关村买。
4. 名人（　　）的产品和名人有关系，才能使广告更有效，比如请姚明为高尔夫球做广告效果肯定不好。
5. 我们的产品刚（　　）的时候，销售量不是很好。
6. 你看今天的新闻了吗？新闻（　　）了我们公司新车发布的事情。
7. 为了吸引更多的消费者，我们（　　）了很多著名的球星来参加我们的活动。
8. 可口可乐公司经常（　　）中国的节日来设计他们的广告。

（二）选择合适的形容词或名词填空。

保修期　惊喜　优惠　激烈　收视率　配置　点子　精美

1. 您是我们的老客户，我们给您报的都是最（　　）的价格。
2. 现在家电行业的竞争越来越（　　）了。
3. 对不起，您的电脑已经过了（　　），我们不能给您免费维修。
4. 那款电脑的价格虽然有点儿贵，可（　　）很不错。
5. 这个电视节目很受大家的喜爱，（　　）非常高。
6. 李平没有把他要回国的事情告诉父母，想给他们一个（　　）。
7. 这种衬衣的包装很好，里面是塑料袋，外面是（　　）的纸盒。
8. 让他帮你出出主意吧，他的（　　）很多。

十、用所给的词完成对话。
Complete the dialogue with the following words.

1. A：我们的副总是法国人，他已经在中国生活了十几年了。

   B：________________________________。（怪不得）

2. A：那个牌子的车挺便宜的，不过性能不是很好。

   B：________________________________。（看来）

3. A：在中央电视台的黄金时段做广告太贵了，怎么办呢？

   B：________________________________。（要不）

4. A：今天上午来面试的人怎么样？有没有合适的？

   B：________________________________。（不怎么样）

5. A：我们的营销方案一定要独特！

   B：对，____________________________。（与众不同）

6. A：听说你们公司最近的销量不是很好，真的吗？

   B：对呀，__________________________。（出主意）

7. A：你觉得怎样才能提高企业的知名度？

   B：____________________________。（要想……就……）

8. A：谁都可以参加你们的抽奖活动吗？

   B：________________________________。（凡）

十一、阅读理解。

Reading comprehension.

如今中国汽车的产销量在迅速上升，未来汽车市场的竞争将会更加激烈，汽车营销将会向网络化、时尚化、个性化和品牌化方向发展。结合多年的市场营销经验，我们总结了今年中国汽车市场的十大营销策略。

最流行——网络营销

如今，报纸、电视、杂志等传统媒体广告市场持续下降，其中相当大的市场份额被网络广告市场所抢占。调查数据显示，中国网民在未来一年购车愿望最强烈。面向都市白领一族的奇瑞QQ在上市前就运用网络定价竞猜游戏，给广大网友带来了惊奇。

最热点——公益营销

CNAJA秘书长李元胜指出，中国汽车营销进入了公益时代，中国汽车企业将会更多地通过公益营销的模式来获得企业、慈善机构、受众群体及客户的多方共赢。一汽的解放车利用公益营销，名利双收。在救灾现场不时穿梭的解放车给观众留下了深刻的印象。

最经济——体育营销

宝马公司很好地利用了体育营销这一利器。超过了35个国家的十多万球员参加的“BMW国际高尔夫杯”，已成为全球最盛大的业余高尔夫赛事。宝马还在莫斯科举办BMW俄罗斯公开赛，在迪拜举办沙漠精英赛等。宝马高尔夫球赛就是这样让开宝马的中国人看起来更优雅。

最高雅——艺术营销

别克为了表达它沉稳内敛和创新进取的个性，别克君威特别赞助了“别克君威大师之夜”暨国际青年钢琴比赛，与11位国际顶级大师共奏洋溢着″动静之美″的华彩乐章。

最实惠——服务营销

在汽车市场竞争日益激烈的今天，有人提出“卖车就是卖服务”。丰田通过点点滴滴为客户着想，将服务营销做到了极致，也赢得了广大消费者的认同。

最省钱——口碑营销

对于目前大多数中国家庭而言，汽车还是昂贵的耐用消费品。而在中高端商务人群中，大部分时间用于参加商务活动，因此，朋友间的口口相传往往成为购买决策的重要依据。据悉，一个好的车型，口碑传播能占销量的30%以上，可以大大地节省广告费和销售成本。

最得民心——责任营销

汽车做为一种便利的交通工具，也给社会带来了一些新的问题。比如尾气排放引发的环境污染和温室效应。汽车企业为了提升自己的形象，实施了环保营销和安全营销策略等责任营销。比如福特设立“福特汽车环保奖”，致力于推动经济和社会的可持续性发展。

最具特色——社区营销

社区营销是中国汽车市场建设的新产物，它摆脱了传统的4S专卖店、大型汽车交易市场或经销商等的束缚。夏夜将汽车搬动到小区广场，让社区居民们试驾，或普及汽车知识，开辟了中国特色的汽车零售渠道。

最吸引人——比附营销

比附营销是一种借助外力来提升自己的附加价值的营销手段。比如车展中比汽车还要受关注的车模就是此类营销中的一种。研究发现，有漂亮车模在旁的汽车比单放的汽车看起来更有价值。

最具突破性——整合营销

整合营销最大的特点是，企业根据消费者的需求特点，将市场进行细分，找到产业的突破口，开拓相对领先的市场，实现品牌的突破，提升产品品牌价值。奇瑞公司运用整合营销理念，准确把握本土市场特点，在产品推广中赢得了市场的热烈反响。

根据上面的这段话回答问题。

1. 汽车营销的趋势是什么？
2. 在汽车市场上，最流行的营销模式是什么？
3. 宝马公司是如何进行体育营销的？
4. 从上文可以知道丰田公司的售后服务怎么样？
5. 运用口碑营销策略能给企业带来什么好处？
6. 上文中提到的“中国特色的汽车零售渠道”是什么？
7. 根据上文，漂亮的车模能否让车看起来更有价值？
8. 你觉得整合营销的特点是什么？

十二、复述课文二。

Retell the text 2.

十三、完成任务。

Complete the following tasks.

1．调查并报告：

请到一些大的超市或是商场参观一下，看看那里有什么促销活动，是怎么做的？回来告诉你的老师和同学。

2．小组讨论：

中国山东的西王玉米油企业是中国最大的玉米油企业，就连中国最大的食用油公司——金龙鱼的玉米油都是由该企业代生产的。他们玉米油的加工工艺先进，品质一流，产品不含胆固醇，对心血管非常有好处。但在食用油市场上他们玉米油的销量并不好，根本没办法跟市场上的花生油、大豆油和调和油相比。你能帮助该企业出一些主意，提高他们的销量吗？几个同学一组，讨论如何帮助这家企业做市场营销。

生词总表 Vocabulary

B

百分点	bǎifēndiǎn	4
百里挑一	bǎilǐtiāoyī	3
搬	bān	6
保修	bǎoxiū	3
保修期	bǎoxiū qī	6
报道	bàodào	6
报销	bàoxiāo	4
抱怨	bàoyuàn	2
被访者	bèifǎngzhě	5
本土	běntǔ	2
本土化	běntǔhuà	2
笔记本电脑	bǐjìběn diànnǎo	6
必备	bìbèi	2
必要	bìyào	5
遍布	biànbù	4
标书	biāoshū	3
并购	bìnggòu	1
不定期	bú dìngqī	1
不断	búduàn	1
不妨	bùfáng	3
部门	bùmén	1

C

参考	cānkǎo	4
参与	cānyǔ	3
策划	cèhuà	1
层次	céngcì	5
差别	chābié	2
差异化	chāyìhuà	6
长线	chángxiàn	3
尝试	chángshì	3
厂商	chǎngshāng	5
畅通	chàngtōng	4
畅销	chàngxiāo	4
炒作	chǎozuò	6
成就	chéngjiù	2
成员	chéngyuán	6
承担	chéngdān	1
程度	chéngdù	5
充分	chōngfèn	5
冲击	chōngjī	4
抽奖	chōu jiǎng	6
初次	chūcì	4
处罚	chǔfá	4
传统	chuántǒng	2

D

达	dá	2

打印机	dǎyìnjī	3
打折	dǎ zhé	6
大胆	dàdǎn	3
大厦	dàshà	6
代理权	dàilǐquán	4
代言	dàiyán	6
道德	dàodé	2
登记证	dēngjìzhèng	3
递交	dìjiāo	3
点子	diǎnzi	6
调整	tiáozhěng	1
定点	dìngdiǎn	5
定额	dìng'é	4
定量	dìngliàng	5
定位	dìngwèi	4
定位	dìngwèi	5
定性	dìngxìng	5
独家	dújiā	4
独立	dúlì	1
独特	dútè	6
对手	duìshǒu	5
对象	duìxiàng	5

F

发布会	fābùhuì	6
发挥	fāhuī	1
发展性消费群	fāzhǎnxìngxiāofèiqún	5
法定	fǎdìng	3
凡	fán	6
反映	fǎnyìng	5
范围	fànwéi	5
方便	fāngbiàn	4
分销	fēnxiāo	2
氛围	fēnwéi	1
份额	fèn'é	5
风土人情	fēngtǔrénqíng	2
服从	fúcóng	2
幅度	fúdù	4
复印机	fùyìnjī	3
副	fù	1
副本	fùběn	3

G

改革	gǎigé	1
改进	gǎijìn	2
概念	gàiniàn	5
干脆	gāncuì	1
感受	gǎnshòu	6
高端	gāoduān	4
搞	gǎo	6
格局	géjú	5
工程师	gōngchéngshī	6
公告	gōnggào	3
功能	gōngnéng	5
供给	gōngjǐ	5
购物中心	gòuwùzhōngxīn	4

关键	guānjiàn	4
关心	guānxīn	2
规模	guīmó	1
规模	guīmó	5
国学	guóxué	2

H

耗材	hàocái	3
合并	hébìng	1
核心消费群	héxīnxiāofèiqún	5
环节	huánjié	1
黄金	huángjīn	6
徽商	huīshāng	2
汇报	huìbào	1

J

及时	jíshí	4
给予	jǐyǔ	4
集中	jízhōng	5
加油	jiāyóu	3
价位	jiàwèi	6
价值观	jiàzhíguān	5
减少	jiǎnshǎo	1
降价	jiàngjià	4
接触	jiēchù	2
接受度	jiēshòudù	4
结构	jiégòu	1
结合	jiéhé	6
结论	jiélùn	5
金额	jīn'é	4
进行	jìnxíng	1
进一步	jìnyíbù	4
晋商	jìnshāng	2
晋升	jìnshēng	2
经销	jīngxiāo	2
惊喜	jīngxǐ	6
精彩	jīngcǎi	6
精美	jīngměi	6
景气	jǐngqì	4
竞标	jìngbiāo	3
竞争者	jìngzhēngzhě	5
俱乐部	jùlèbù	6
决策	juécè	5
决策	juécè	1
绝对	juéduì	2
君子爱财	jūnzǐ'àicái	2

K

开标	kāibiāo	3
开发	kāifā	1
开拓	kāituò	4
看重	kànzhòng	3
苛刻	kēkè	3
科学	kēxué	5
可取之处	kěqǔzhīchù	2
可行性	kěxíngxìng	5
客户群	kèhùqún	4
口味	kǒuwèi	2
款	kuǎn	6

L

老	lǎo	2
礼包	lǐbāo	6
利润	lìrùn	1

流程	liúchéng	1
论坛	lùntán	6

M

梦寐以求	mèngmèiyǐqiú	1
弥补	míbǔ	3
民营	mínyíng	2
名人	míngrén	6
明显	míngxiǎn	2

N

难得	nándé	1

P

牌子	páizi	6
培训	péixùn	1
培养	péiyǎng	1
配额	pèi'é	5
配置	pèizhì	6
品种	pǐnzhǒng	2
破产	pòchǎn	1

Q

期间	qījiān	6
期望	qīwàng	5
企划	qǐhuà	5
启发	qǐfā	6
起码	qǐmǎ	3
洽谈	qiàtán	4
潜力	qiánlì	1
潜在	qiánzài	5
潜在消费群	qiánzàixiāofèiqún	5
强烈	qiángliè	2
强项	qiángxiàng	4
轻松	qīngsōng	5
取消	qǔxiāo	1
取之有道	qǔzhīyǒudào	2
全面	quánmiàn	1

R

人群	rénqún	5
人性化	rénxìnghuà	2
仍然	réngrán	4
日益	rìyì	4
容量	róngliàng	5
儒家	rújiā	2
儒商	rúshāng	2
入迷	rùmí	3
入选	rùxuǎn	2
软文	ruǎnwén	6

S

散会	sànhuì	5
商人	shāngrén	2
上门服务	shàngménfúwù	3
上市	shàngshì	6
上司	shàngsi	2
上涨	shàngzhǎng	4
舍得	shěde	1
升级	shēngjí	5
十足	shízú	3
时段	shíduàn	6

时尚	shíshàng	4
实力	shílì	4
实习	shíxí	1
实行	shíxíng	2
市场部	shìchǎngbù	5
市场调研	shìchǎng diàoyán	1
事业部	shìyèbù	1
事宜	shìyí	4
试驾	shìjià	6
收购	shōugòu	1
收视率	shōushì lǜ	6
授权	shòuquán	3
书面	shūmiàn	3
舒适性	shūshìxìng	6
数据	shùjù	5
税务	shuìwù	3
思想	sīxiǎng	2
送	sòng	6

T

讨价还价	tǎojiàhuánjià	3
提升	tíshēng	1
体验	tǐyàn	5
替代	tìdài	5
跳槽	tiàocáo	1
通行	tōngxíng	5
统计	tǒngjì	5
头脑	tóunǎo	3
头疼	tóuténg	2
投标	tóubiāo	3
投标人	tóubiǎorén	3
投放	tóufàng	6
团队合作	tuánduì hézuò	1
推出	tuīchū	2
拓展训练	tuòzhǎn xùnliàn	1

W

外包	wàibāo	2
网络	wǎngluò	4
维修	wéixiū	3
委托	wěituō	5
问卷	wènjuàn	5

X

细分	xìfēn	5
下调	xiàtiáo	4
现身说法	xiànshēnshuōfǎ	6
现状	xiànzhuàng	5
消费群体	xiāofèiqúntǐ	5
销售量	xiāoshòu liàng	1
欣赏	xīnshǎng	1
性能	xìngnéng	6
需求	xūqiú	2
需求	xūqiú	5
需求量	xūqiúliàng	5
序言	xùyán	5
宣传	xuānchuán	4
选定	xuǎndìng	5

Y

压	yā	3
严格	yángé	2
研发	yánfā	1
眼下	yǎnxià	5

样本	yàngběn	5
邀请	yāoqǐng	6
业绩	yèjì	3
一等奖	yīděngjiǎng	6
移动硬盘	yídòngyìngpán	6
以便	yǐbiàn	5
意识	yìshí	1
意向	yìxiàng	3
因素	yīnsù	4
引导	yǐndǎo	6
引领	yǐnlíng	4
盈利	yínglì	2
营业	yíngyè	3
佣金	yòngjīn	4
用户	yònghù	5
优秀	yōuxiù	2
与众不同	yǔzhòngbùtóng	6
预审	yùshěn	3
运用	yùnyòng	2

Z

责任	zérèn	1
责任感	zérèn'gǎn	2
增加	zēngjiā	1
赠送	zèngsòng	6
展厅	zhǎntīng	6
占有率	zhànyǒulǜ	5
招标	zhāobiāo	3
针对	zhēnduì	4
争取	zhēngqǔ	4
整合	zhěnghé	1
之	zhī	2
知己知彼	zhījǐ zhībǐ	5
知名度	zhīmíngdù	4
执照	zhízhào	3
智慧	zhìhuì	2
置信度	zhìxìndù	5
中标	zhòngbiāo	3
中国通	zhōngguótōng	2
中奖率	zhòngjiǎnglǜ	6
重大	zhòngdà	5
重点	zhòngdiǎn	5
重视	zhòngshì	1
重组	chóngzǔ	1
主流	zhǔliú	5
主体	zhǔtǐ	5
注重	zhùzhòng	4
专访	zhuānfǎng	6
专家	zhuānjiā	5
专业	zhuānyè	5
赚	zhuàn	3
状况	zhuàngkuàng	5
准确度	zhǔnquèdù	5
着手	zhuóshǒu	3
资格	zīgé	3
资源	zīyuán	1
总裁	zǒngcái	1
组织	zǔzhī	1

专有名词总表
Proper Nouns

2 摩托罗拉
Mótuōluólā
Motorola Inc.

2 惠普
Huìpǔ
HP, Hewlett-Packard Development Company, L.P.

2 肯德基
Kěndéjī
KFC(Kentucky Fried Chicken)

2 日企
Rìqǐ
Japanese enterprises

日本企业（全称）
Rìběn qǐyè

2 韩国
Hánguó
The Republic of Korea

2 荷兰皇家壳牌（集团）
Hélán Huángjiā Qiàopái（Jítuán）
Royal Dutch /Shell Group of Companies

2 沃尔玛
Wò'ěrmǎ
Wal-Mart Stores, Inc.

2 中石化
hōngshíhuà
Sinopec Group

中国石油化工集团（全称）
Zhōngguó Shíyóu Huàgōng Jítuán
China Petro-chemical Corporation

2 《孙子兵法》
《Sūnzǐ Bīngfǎ》
The Art of War

3 市政府
Shìzhèngfǔ
Municipal government

3 招标委员会
Zhāobiāo Wěiyuánhuì
Tender Board

4 宏图公司
Hóngtú Gōngsī
Hongtu Company

6 中关村
ZhōngGuānCūn
Zhongguancun, an avenue is located in Haidian District of Beijing

6 海龙大厦
HǎiLóng DàShà
Hailong Tower, Electronics Tower

6 新马泰
Xīn Mǎ Tài
abbreviation of Singapore, Malaysia, Thailand